D1370764

THE SATURDAY EVENING POST

Antioxidant
Cookbook

THE SATURDAY EVENING POST

Antioxidant Cookbook

CORY SERVAAS, M.D.

Benjamin Franklin Literary & Medical Society
Indianapolis, Indiana 46202

The Saturday Evening Post
Antioxidant Cookbook

Patrick Perry, *Managing Editor*
Patti Olson, R.D., *Food Editor*
Jolie SerVaas, Walter Mathews,
Charlotte Turgeon, *Contributing Editors*
Phyllis Lybarger, *Typesetting/Layout*
Chris Wilhoite, *Art Director*
Dwight Lamb, *Production Manager*
Jack Merritt, *Book Division*
Jean Browning Rose, *Consulting Editor*
Jean White, *Assistant Editor*
Michael Hayes, *Design Consultant*

Special thanks to Charlotte Turgeon, Walter Mathews, and the staff of
The Saturday Evening Post *magazine for their invaluable recipe and editorial contributions.*

Copyright © 1995 by The Saturday Evening Post Society. All rights reserved.
No part of this book may be used or reproduced in any manner whatsoever without written
permission except in the case of brief quotations embodied in critical articles and reviews.
Published in Nashville, Tennessee, by Thomas Nelson, Inc., and distributed in Canada by
Word Communications, Ltd., Richmond, British Columbia, and in the
United Kingdom by Word (UK), Ltd., Milton Keynes, England.
Printed in The United States of America.
For information, address: The Saturday Evening Post Society,
1100 Waterway Boulevard, Indianapolis, Indiana 46202.

ISBN 0-7852-75118
ISBN 0-7852-75096
ISBN 0-7852-75126

1 2 3 4 5 6 7 - 0 1 0 0 9 9 9 8 9 7 9 6 9 5

Contents

Foreword

Editor's note: Nobel prize-winning chemist Linus Pauling, Ph.D., wrote the following introduction to The Vitamin C Cookbook, *which was published in 1975. Twenty years later, Pauling's belief in the effectiveness of vitamin C and the use of vitamins to prevent disease continues to gain ground in scientific circles. When we spoke with him before he died at age 93, Pauling was still stirring 16 grams of vitamin C into his orange juice daily. His lifelong advocacy of antioxidants as an invaluable ally in mankind's battle against disease was recorded by* The Saturday Evening Post. *When Dr. Pauling first told us how he poured crystalline vitamin C into his morning glass of orange juice, we wanted to share his practice with as many people as possible. It was Dr. Pauling's original idea that prompted us to produce a vitamin C cookbook, giving people who might not drink orange juice other ways to augment the vitamin C content of their food, thus avoiding the need for swallowing capsules or tablets. It seemed fitting to invite Dr. Pauling to write an introduction to the cookbook. He promptly sent us the following.*

Our food contains many substances that are required for life and good health—proteins (including the essential amino acids), carbohydrates, essential fats, vitamins, and the essential minerals. The state of our health depends on the amounts of these substances that we ingest. There is much evidence to support the belief that the health of most people is improved by the intake of larger amounts of vitamin C (L-ascorbic acid) than those usually provided in the modern diet. A good way to obtain these large amounts is by incorporating extra vitamin C in foods as they are being prepared for the table. Dr. Cory SerVaas and her collaborator, Walter Mathews, have written their book, *The Vitamin C Cookbook*, to help people achieve better health in this way.

In 1974 the Food and Nutrition Board of the United States National Academy of Science—National Research Council set the Recommended Dietary Allowance (RDA) for vitamin C at 45 milligrams per day. This value is less than the 60 milligrams per day that the

Board had set in 1968 and the still earlier 75 milligrams per day that the Board had set in 1958. Many people receive 45 milligrams per day in their ordinary food, but many others, those whose diets are not well selected, do not.

We may ask whether the RDA recommendation is adequate. The Food and Nutrition Board says that it is adequate to prevent scurvy in most people, and I agree that it is. On the other hand, I believe, as do Irwin Stone, Roger J. Williams, and some other scientists, that it is not adequate to put people in the best of health.

Roger J. Williams, who discovered one of the B vitamins (pantothenic acid), has evidence that people differ from one another in their need for vitamin C, as well as other nutrients. My estimate is that the optimum rate of intake of vitamin C—the intake that puts a person in the best of health—lies between 1 gram (1,000 milligrams) and 10 grams per day for most people. Irwin Stone recommends about 3 grams per day.

If you stop eating foods rich in vitamin C, you should take the equivalent amount of vitamin C as tablets. It is important to keep to a regular intake of the vitamin because it is not stored in very large quantities in the body. The body adjusts to a high rate of intake of vitamin C by converting much of it into other substances, which may themselves be useful. If you suddenly stop the large intake, the body continues to convert the remaining vitamin C into the other substances for a little while, a couple of weeks, and then the body level of the vitamin drops below that required for good protection against disease.

Vitamin C is a valuable substance. A mixed diet of raw natural plant foods would provide an adult with over 2,000 milligrams of this valuable substance each day. Modern diets, unsupplemented, provide far less. The deficit may be made up by taking extra vitamin C, perhaps as described in the recipes in this book.

Linus Pauling, Ph.D.
Linus Pauling Institute of Science and Medicine
Menlo Park, California
1975

Introduction

Scan a newspaper or watch television and you will undoubtedly see or hear the words *antioxidant* or *free radicals*. In many ways, they have become the nutrition buzzwords of the '90s.

Everyone on earth relies on stable oxygen—it is essential for life. Free radicals, however, are unstable oxygen molecules seeking out other molecules with which to combine. Our bodies combat free radicals with a natural checks-and-balances system—antioxidants. Antioxidants keep free radicals in check, preventing them from damaging our bodies. Unfortunately, today's world exposes us to more free radicals than our bodies can handle naturally. Exposure to ultraviolet light, pesticides, cigarette smoke, air pollution, and contaminants in our food results in an overabundance of free radicals in our bodies. Scientists are increasingly linking these free radicals to a wide range of diseases: cancer, heart disease, cataracts, arthritis, and other illnesses.

How can we protect ourselves from the free-radical threat? To counteract the imbalance in our bodies, we must bolster our natural antioxidant defense system. Not long ago, many physicians in the medical community opposed taking supplemental vitamins, believing our daily diet provided all the vitamins and minerals needed. However, substantial research into free radicals and antioxidants has created an about face in mainstream medicine. *The Saturday Evening Post* editors are proud to have been tracking and reporting on antioxidants and free radicals for the past twenty years. In 1976 we attended the 83rd birthday party for Dr. Albert Szent-Györgyi, the discoverer of vitamin C (ascorbic acid). Dr. and Mrs. Linus Pauling were in Boston for this glorious birthday celebration. For readers who joined the Saturday Evening Post Society more recently, we should explain that Dr. Szent-Györgyi lost his wife and daughter to breast cancer when he was still a young man. He spent the rest of his long life researching the cause of cancer.

Since our introduction into the promising antioxidant/free radical link to cancer and disease prevention in the '70s, we've observed various specialities in medicine, one by one, taking a renewed interest in antioxidants.

We were sufficiently impressed with Dr. Szent-Györgyi's theories to begin writing *The Vitamin C Cookbook,* and we asked Dr. Linus Pauling to write the introduction.

Doubleday agreed to publish *The Vitamin C Cookbook* in 1975. We have updated the book to include more recent research information about the importance of the antioxidants beta carotene and vitamin E. Vitamin E is a stronger antioxidant than vitamin C, but "C" helps to recycle vitamin E in the body. Vitamin E and beta carotene recipes have been added to augment the original vitamin C chapters.

Although evidence supporting the need for supplemental vitamins is emerging, diet remains the cornerstone of the body's nutrient requirements. High-fiber, antioxidant-rich foods provide a strong base on which to build a powerful natural defense system.

We like the idea of supplying the vitamin C in foods because, unlike vitamin E, vitamin C is water-soluble and flushes out of the body quickly. Dr. Kenneth Cooper, pioneer of aerobics, now leads the crusade for the antioxidant revolution. He recommends taking vitamin C twice daily. Having a vitamin C shaker on the table instead of a salt shaker might be a healthier habit for all of us.

Recipes for Healthy Living

Filled with delicious recipes high in beta carotene, vitamin C, and vitamin E, this cookbook offers easy-to-follow, easy-to-prepare menu ideas, as well as tips on how to get the most antioxidants from the foods you eat. The *Antioxidant Cookbook* provides today's health-conscious consumer with a user-friendly tool to maximize the chances of enjoying the best of health.

Don't suppose for a minute that this cookbook sacrifices the taste, texture, color, character, spice, or spirit of fine dining on some sterile altar of "healthy eating through chemistry." Certainly not! *The Saturday Evening Post Antioxidant Cookbook* offers a felicitous blend of delicious recipes basted with the good sense of responsible eating through the application of groundbreaking scientific research. Each recipe has been carefully selected to evoke the culinary senses, delight the palate, and satisfy the appetites and sensuous pleasures of diners of taste.

In addition, recipes include salient information on selection, healthy preparation, and storage of individual ingredients and leftover portions. At the beginning of each recipe, you will find the content of vitamin C in milligrams. Recipes with significant beta carotene and/or vitamin E content are marked with a ☆. Following each recipe, you will find technical calculations of the nutrients supplied by a single serving. Note, too, that portions are small. Healthy food, tastefully prepared and attractively presented, satisfies and thus curbs the tendency to overeat.

The Antioxidant Heroes: Vitamins C, E, and Beta Carotene

Vitamin C exists in varying amounts in many fruits and vegetables (see Appendix). Papaya, oranges, grapefruit, strawberries, cantaloupe, guava, and cranberry juice are excellent sources of vitamin C. So, too, are vegetables such as tomatoes, broccoli, Brussels sprouts, cauliflower, and potatoes. Vitamin C, a water-soluble vitamin, is important in fighting infections, including the common cold. The body also requires vitamin C to build and maintain bone, cartilage, dentin, collagen, and connective tissue in general.

Vitamin E, a fat-soluble vitamin, is not as easily found in ample supply in our everyday foods (see Appendix). For example, one quarter cup diced almonds contains only 7.5 mg of D-alpha tocopheral, while one sweet potato contains 5.93 mg. For purposes of comparison, 1 mg is equal to 1 International Unit (IU) of vitamin E. The minimum recommended daily amount of E, however, is 10 mg for men and 8 mg for women. Specialists have recommended levels closer to 30 IU. It is quickly apparent that you would have to consume enormous amounts of vitamin E-rich foods to reach this amount. For that reason, you should include a vitamin E supplement in your daily regimen.

Vitamin E helps to counteract the deleterious effects of cigarette smoke and other harmful environmental pollutants. It is effective in reducing the size of benign breast cysts, and it helps in the treatment of sickle cell anemia and infant blindness. In general, vitamin E protects cellular and subcellular membranes.

Beta carotene, the "provitamin" or precursor vitamin A, is best acquired by eating such fruits and vegetables as pumpkin, spinach, carrots, cantaloupes, broccoli, and mangoes (see Appendix). Vitamin A is important in the formation of epithelial tissue, found in skin, glands, mucous membrane, and all along the respiratory and gastrointestinal tracts. Beta carotene provides protection against cancer, heart disease, stroke, and cataracts. The vitamin A source may be listed as International Units (IU), Retinol Equivalents (RE), or micrograms from plants and animal sources. For purposes of comparison, 1 microgram RE is equal to 6 micrograms beta carotene from plant sources or 1 microgram non-beta carotene (retinol) from animal sources.

Storage and Preparation

Factors such as exposure to light, heat, and oxygen cause antioxidants to deteriorate. Fresh vegetables should be stored in moisture-proof bags in the refrigerator or freezer. Wilted vegetables lose considerable amounts of vitamin C and beta carotene. Cutting, trimming, slicing, and chopping fruits and vegetables exposes the surfaces to the ravages of oxygen and temperature changes. Foods containing "C" and beta carotene also lose potency when exposed to water in the washing process during the preparation of a meal. Care should be taken to use fruits and vegetables as soon after purchase as possible.

Using excessive heat in the cooking process also damages antioxidants. To best preserve vitamins, steam, stir-fry, or microwave foods. Reuse the water in which you have cooked vegetables; it can be a good source of antioxidants. Avoid frying because it destroys many of the nutrients in vegetables. Serve foods within 30 minutes after cooking. Do not use precut produce, and don't store produce in the refrigerator more than a few days.

Finally, enjoy the recipes in the *Antioxidant Cookbook*, knowing that they are not only delicious, but also nutritious.

Cory SerVaas, M.D.
Editor-in-Chief
The Saturday Evening Post

The Story of Antioxidants

Before we so much as touch a skillet or wave a whisk in the air, we'd like you to know why we add antioxidant vitamins C, E, and beta carotene to our own diets, and why we think you should. We'd like to arouse your curiosity about these powerful natural nutrients so the fascination of nutrition research will capture your imagination. The more you learn about the important role nutrition has played in the histories of nations, the more intrigued you will become with your own "kitchen power."

Most of all, although we certainly hope that your adventure with vitamins will be fun and have the small excitements that all excursions into new culinary fields bring, we want you to realize for yourself and your family certain very serious goals we have set by adopting the use of antioxidants in so many enjoyable phases of eating.

The first is to eat better. The renewal of our appetites is a daily blessing and one which only spoilsports do not appreciate. The cooking techniques in our recipes, as well as the recipes themselves, have been carefully planned and researched to extract the very fullest and richest flavors from all ingredients.

The second goal is to feel better. Vitamin C, as we shall learn a little later on, has only recently been understood, in the long history of humanity, as one of the great natural benefits available to us. Our second goal, then, is to provide maximum retention of "C" in addition to providing maximum retention of the other natural ingredients. We then counsel you in ways to add a more sensible amount of vitamin C, vitamin E, and beta carotene so as to maximize this natural insurance to your health. Many recipes have vitamin C in the ingredients to start with, but many will add "C" (vitamin C) in palatable amounts as well; the resulting amount per serving is given at the top of the recipes.

The third goal is to spend less. This book endeavors to be contemporary in its economy, as well as in its other counsel. We're not going to skimp a bit on taste or quality, but we are going to use less-expensive ingredients when possible and tell you ways of using practically all of the food you buy.

Vitamin C (ascorbic acid) is an essential nutrient that the body does not manufacture or store. So that you will get vitamin C easily and regularly, we are putting it where it belongs—in the kitchen as a food and as a responsibility of the cook.

Our cookbook is written to provide you with tested recipes telling you how to add powdered or crystalline vitamin C so you may eliminate vitamin C tablets and still provide yourself and your family with as much vitamin C as you wish for your maximum good health. We hope that, before long, vitamin C will be as common an ingredient in your kitchen cabinet as flour, sugar, or iodized salt.

Taking an essential nutrient and removing it from the "drug" category by putting it into your kitchen armamentarium has been done before now. Iodized salt is one example. Our salt box is labeled "Iodized salt—a necessary nutrient," and the label is correct. At one time simple goiters (enlarged thyroid glands) were prevalent because of an iodine deficiency in food and drinking water. "Goiter belts" were found in mountainous regions around the world, as well as in the Great Lakes region of the United States.

A deficiency of iodine in the diet prevents the formation of sufficient thyroid hormone and leads to pituitary stimulation of the thyroid gland and, thus, its enlargement. Unsightly, thick, swollen necks from simple goiters were a common sight, and mentally disabled ("cretin") children were frequently born in areas where these goiters were prevalent.

Then, in 1924, thanks to the efforts of the Michigan Medical Association, a salt-packaging company was prevailed upon to add potassium iodide to their table salt. Simple goiters became virtually a thing of the past.

What a nuisance it would be if all of us had to take iodine pills to keep some of us from getting simple iodine-deficiency goiters. If, as many believe, vitamin C is a healthful supplement to our daily diets, it, too, should become as common a part of our cooking and eating as adding iodized salt once was.

Pure vitamin C in powder or crystalline form is available from a number of sources, and it is easy to include in your cooking. You may want to increase the vitamin C intake for individual members of your family under varying conditions. It seems relatively certain that the body requires greater amounts of vitamin C when under nervous or physical stress. We know that wound and burn healing is enhanced by vitamin C. Illness seems to create a greater need for vitamin C, as does smoking. Smokers, on the average, destroy 25 milligrams of vitamin C with each cigarette smoked—which means they'd have to eat half an orange after each cigarette just to stay even with nonsmokers. Most patients with bladder tumors are smokers. To prevent recurrence of bladder tumors, many urologists administer 1,500 milligrams of vitamin C per day to all patients who have developed such tumors.

Much interesting research is currently under way on vitamin C. Some years ago, several English physicians argued that vitamin C was beneficial in preventing coronary vascular disease—a belief gaining momentum in scientific circles today.

A few doctors theorize that pharmacological doses of vitamin C can combat viral diseases of all kinds. Still others combine vitamin C with the amino acid L-lysine and proclaim positive results in fighting the Epstein-Barr virus and chronic fatigue syndrome.

The list goes on. Small wonder that the public has become intrigued with the honest differences of opinion among researchers. It is fortunate for us that there is controversy, for it stimulates further research.

The wheels of research turn slowly—it takes time to verify and repeat, to wait and see. The half-life of medical knowledge is often quoted to be only eight years; in other words, one half of everything that we now believe to be true in medicine will have been proved wrong or obsolete in eight years. So keep your eyes open. Be skeptical—and make a few investigations of your own. Trust neither the doubting Thomases who resist changes nor the overly enthusiastic.

Years ago, medical schools taught that if we ate a balanced diet, we shouldn't need to take vitamins. This is now being refuted by most of their alumni. As the iodized-salt story illustrates, old concepts are often proved erroneous. If the public and the medical profession had been more diet-conscious, we probably would have discovered earlier that the thousands of our forebears who were going around with "tired blood" were really suffering from the lack of iodine in the drinking water and soil of their region. This deficiency simply left them without enough thyroid hormone to feel peppy—but with enough of it to prevent a telltale goiter. In other words, those goiters were probably just the beginning. Resting in their graves are probably countless prematurely weary souls and their retarded children—all because it took us until 1924 to add iodine to our salt.

But medical research in our generation is racing along at jet speed compared with the snail's pace of only a few generations back. Consider, for example, the time it took to eliminate death from scurvy in England. Vitamin C made it possible for Britain, using its unsurpassed sea power, to become the foremost nation on earth. Simply by sucking vitamin C from a lime, British sailors—thenceforth known as "limeys"—conquered scurvy, the ball and chain that had shackled the world's navies close to their home ports.

Nearly everyone has read stories of sailors dying of scurvy on long voyages far away from the fresh viands of the land and countryside. In 1497, Vasco da Gama, while discovering a new sea route to India, lost 100 of his 160-man crew to scurvy. In 1740, Commodore Anson sailed from England with six ships and 1,500 men; four years later, when he crept back to port, scurvy had cut his force to one ship and 335 men.

Dr. James Lind, a Scottish physician in the British naval service, discovered citrus to be a cure for scurvy in 1747, but it took more than forty years for the British Admiralty to adopt the practice of supplying each sailor with a daily ration of one ounce of juice from the lime. The Admiralty never did know why lime juice stopped scurvy; they only knew that it did.

For more than a hundred years after the Royal Navy learned to take care of its "limeys" and England became a seagoing power, civilian ships in the British Merchant Marine were still sailing without any fruit aboard. Many thought, in fact, that it was the highly salted, dried foods eaten by soldiers and sailors that caused the scurvy—not the lack of nutriment.

This general ignorance extended on land to the armies, which went on eating only their customary salted meat and hardtack, suffering and dying from scurvy.

And the English weren't the only ones at fault. The United States managed to lose 30,000 soldiers to scurvy as late as the Civil War—all for want of a little lime juice in their rations.

In retrospect, scientist-journalist Benjamin Franklin was probably too busy fighting for vaccinations against the more dramatic deaths from scarlet fever in his day. Later, leading publicist-writer-physician Dr. Oliver Wendell Holmes would have surely attacked the lack of scurvy prophylaxis if he hadn't been so preoccupied with crusading against childbed fever deaths from unclean hands in delivery rooms.

It was not until the beginning of this century that any real progress was made toward isolating and identifying vitamin C as ascorbic acid and ascertaining its many sources. In the early 1930s, Dr. Albert Szent-Györgyi discovered vitamin C. For that discovery, he was awarded the Nobel Prize in 1937.

Simply stated, vitamin C is essential to life, affecting virtually every part of the body. We cannot live without it. Furthermore, the human body, unlike that of most animals, cannot manufacture its own vitamin C. (Humans are one of a handful of living species deprived of an enzyme we once possessed—a shortcoming we share with monkeys, guinea pigs, and only a few other rare living things.) We must obtain vitamin C, therefore, from the things we eat, and we need continual replenishment of it because our bodies are also unable to store it.

How much do we need daily? No one knows for sure. We do know that a relatively small amount, just 35 milligrams per day, will prevent scurvy. Dr. Albert Szent-Györgyi himself considered 35 milligrams too modest a goal:

> *"Scurvy is not the first sign of the deficiency, but a premortal syndrome, and for full health you need much more, very much more. I am taking, myself, about one gram a day. This does not mean that this is really the optimum dose because we do not know what full health really means and how much ascorbic acid you need for it. What I can tell you is that one can take any amount of ascorbic acid without the least danger."*

(Dr. Szent-Györgyi lived to the ripe old age of ninety-two.)

Another Nobel Prize winner, nonagenarian Dr. Linus Pauling, added this:

> *"It may be a long time before we know what the optimum intake rate of this important food is. There is no doubt that it varies from person to person. . . . I am sure that an increased intake of ascorbic acid, 10 to 100 times the daily allowance of*

60 milligrams per day recommended by the Food and Nutrition Board, leads to the improvement of general health and to increased resistance to infectious disease. It is my opinion that for most people, the optimum daily intake is somewhere between 250 milligrams and 10 grams."

For certain of you, it is appropriate to seek the advice of your physician before including large amounts of vitamin C or large amounts of any other nutriment in your diet. If you are pregnant or diabetic, your diet, of course, should be supervised by your own physician. Vitamin C acidifies the urine and thus prevents the most common kinds of kidney stones, which are alkaline based. However, there is an extremely rare kind of stone that forms more easily in an acid urine. If you should be one of the rare individuals in whom this condition exists, you can still consume high levels of vitamin C if you choose, but you should be taking sodium ascorbate instead of the ascorbic acid. Sodium ascorbate is readily available, but if you are on a low-salt diet, you will want to be guided by the advice of your own physician. People on low-salt diets should not consume large amounts of sodium ascorbate—or sodium bicarbonate, either, for that matter.

We asked Dr. Milton Helpern, renowned former chief medical examiner for the City of New York, why he took vitamin C. His answer was direct: "Because Linus Pauling does." Further questioning disclosed that he had made a few observations himself. He noted that the lesions of atherosclerosis in the blood vessels resemble the lesions of scurvy. Because he's probably done more autopsies than any other man alive, such a remark coming from him should encourage further investigation.

If modern researchers turn out to be right and scurvy proves to be just the tip of the vitamin C iceberg, history will only be repeating itself. We hope we may all live to know the truth.

And if anyone is too complacent in assuring you that you can "forget the vitamins if you eat 'normally balanced meals'," you might suggest that one need only look at our increasingly high incidence of cancer and coronary-vascular disease to know that we may be doing or eating something wrong . . . or perhaps not eating something our species needs to survive during the next 10,000 years. If evolution has played tricks on us by omitting an enzyme or two along the way, it may be best to keep open minds to find the answers before it's too late. If one out of four of us is now destined to have cancer, and one out of three of us is destined to die from coronary-vascular disease, perhaps the trend is sufficiently alarming to make medical observers of us all. Future generations may well look back upon us, shaking their heads and wondering why it took us so long.

Where You Find Vitamin C

There are two easily available sources of vitamin C—natural and synthetic, both of which are of equal value to us. Vitamin C in its natural state is an example of nature's well-known quixotic generosity on the one hand and indifference on the other. Some foods have a lot of it; others have none at all. It is found most abundantly in fruits and vegetables. Vitamin C is practically nonexistent in dairy products. It does not exist in grains, nuts, baked goods, or in beverages such as coffee, tea, alcohol in fermented grain libations, wine, or unsupplemented carbonated drinks. Unless a dessert has fruits in it, no amount of artistry can induce much vitamin C to lurk there. The only meats containing any significant amount of vitamin C are animal livers, where it is stored for the animal's sustenance.

In the Appendix, you will find a chart of vitamin C content in natural food sources. Synthesized vitamin C is derived from glucose, a form of sugar. It is pure ascorbic acid, and we find it easy to use for cooking because it is rapidly soluble. One form is powdered vitamin C; another is in crystalline form. You can use either.

We want you to think of vitamin C as a food—not a chemical or a drug. Observe its molecular structure (see diagram following page) and you will see how closely it resembles glucose. The chemical formula for ascorbic acid is $C_6H_8O_6$; glucose is $C_6H_{12}O_6$. Ascorbic acid simply contains four fewer atoms of hydrogen in a slightly different arrangement. And don't let the name *ascorbic acid* worry you. After all, table salt is sodium chloride, baking soda is sodium carbonate, and cream of tartar is potassium bitartrate. We've been using these ingredients in the kitchen since our great-grandmothers were girls.

If a chemist were given two containers of vitamin C, one synthesized (starting with glucose) and the other natural vitamin C taken from fresh oranges or vegetables, he would not be able to distinguish the two substances chemically by any known tests. We point this out because we believe synthesized vitamin C, the cheapest form available, is as good as any product advertised as "natural" vitamin C.

Ascorbic Acid   Glucose

Both the powder and the crystals are chemically indistinguishable from the vitamin C found in oranges and vegetables. It is in concentrated form, labeled "Ascorbic Acid, U.S.P., Fine Crystals" or "Ascorbic Acid, U.S.P., Powder." The recipes in this book are based on the use of a U.S. standard measuring spoon. One such teaspoon of crystalline vitamin C will weigh 4,000 milligrams. If you buy the powdered form, which is fluffier, you should use a slightly rounded measuring spoonful to give the equivalent weight.

You will find that an ordinary dining room teaspoon will usually hold approximately 3,000 milligrams of crystalline vitamin C.

There's one source of vitamin C that comes under the luxury category. It is vitamin C advertised as "all natural" and produced commercially from rose hips. (These are the fruits that are left when the petals fall off the flower.) It comes in various forms, including liquid. It is true that rose hips have extremely high concentration of vitamin C. However, the quality of the "C" from rose hips is no better than that from any other source and is usually far more expensive.

Of course, you may buy vitamin C in tablet form, and many do. The tablets are usually much more expensive than the crystalline or powder form, and they often contain filler you don't need. For example, a sample cost comparison yielded the following results:

A commonly sold brand of 250 milligram pills in a bottle containing 100 pills costs $5.25.

100 pills x 250 mg	= 25,000 mg
cost for 25,000 mg	= $5.25
cost per 1,000 mg	= .21
cost per day of 4 members in family taking 1,000 mg per day	= $0.84

Whereas in the crystalline or powder:

8 oz. x 28,350 mg per oz.	= 226,800 mg
cost for 226,800 mg	= $11.00
cost per 1,000 mg	= approx. 5¢
cost per day of 4 members in family taking 1,000 mg per day	= $ .20

In this case, the pills cost more than 4 times as much as the crystals.

Nevertheless, there is the matter of convenience. If you eat frequently or regularly in restaurants or away from home, and if there is no other way to obtain all the vitamin C you want from your food, you may need to use tablets. If so, use larger ones (500 milligrams or 1000 milligrams). They usually cost less than smaller ones and contain less filler.

For the recipes in this book, obtain vitamin C powder or crystals. It is commercially produced under rigorous government regulations and is uniformly the same, whatever the price. Comparison-shop for vitamin C. We found one store selling 8 ounces of the crystalline form for $15.99; in another, 4 ounces cost $6.00. Same product, different name brands, so do look around a bit. If you cannot find crystalline or powder vitamin C, don't hesitate to ask your druggist to order it for you. If tablets must be used, crush them well before adding to the recipes. Twenty 100 milligram tablets will be equivalent to a half measuring teaspoon of ascorbic acid crystals.

Cooking with Vitamin C

We've come to the point where, we hope, you're now beginning to think of vitamin C as just another staple around the kitchen—one that spruces up the flavor of what you are cooking and offers a possible health insurance none of us can afford to ignore. So keep it on your favorite shelf, next to the sage and the peppercorns.

Our aim now is to tell you about the most pleasant and economical ways to cook with "C." First, some general notes:

1. Vitamin C deteriorates when exposed to air, light, and high

temperatures, so we have added "C" at the end of most recipes. When food containing vitamin C is stored, it should be refrigerated and protected from air as much as possible.

2. Because vitamin C dissolves into the water, as little water as possible is used, unless the liquid itself is part of the recipe (soups, for example).

3. Copper and iron have a deleterious effect on vitamin C. Do not use utensils made of either (unless they are coated with something else).

4. Method of preparation is important in determing retention of vitamin C in foods. To help you understand how varying techniques of preparation can actually reduce vitamin C content in foods originally rich in the substance, let's take the example of the potato.

Studies at the Nutrition Laboratory of Yale University School of Medicine were made to determine the effect of various cooking methods on retention of vitamins (including "C") and minerals in 12 vegetables. Four different methods were used: waterless, pressure cooking, using a half cup of water per 100 grams, and cooking with water to cover.

Assuming that raw potatoes have 100 percent of their vitamin C intact, cooking with water to cover them will reduce that vitamin C content to 41.0 percent of what they contained when raw. The remaining vitamin content rises slightly to 48.4 percent when you use one half cup of water, and to 57.3 percent when pressure cooked. However, when prepared "waterless" or baked, the percentage of vitamin C retained is 79.4 percent.

The Yale study emphasizes one point of interest—of all the vitamins studied, the percentage loss of vitamin C was greater than that of any other vitamin in every method of cooking.

This is only part of what happens to vitamin C in the potato on its way to the table. When potatoes are first harvested, they actually contain many times as much vitamin C as they do later. Losses during storage approximate one quarter of the vitamin C content after one month, one half after three months, and three quarters after nine months. When we consider that the growing seasons in Maine and Idaho, our two main areas for potato production, are strictly summer seasonal, we can reflect that purchase of new potatoes is a factor in our intake of vitamin C.

For the recipes in this book, we have used fresh ingredients because they taste better. When cooked carefully, they are often more nutritious and, in season, are usually less expensive than the canned variety.

If you wish to use canned substitutes, by all means do so. You may also use commercially frozen foods. Better still, take advantage of our chapter on "Home Freezing of Fruits."

We hope this book will be successful in showing you how to use vitamin C and other antioxidants to enrich the bounty that nature has already stored in fruits, vegetables, and liver. We want you to discover ways of using vitamin C in the preparation of meats, fish, and poultry, which have so many other nutritional elements for us.

We hope that this adventure with antioxidants will be fun, exciting, and a major nutritional discovery for your diet.

And so, as we move into this fresh approach to an age-old benefice, we borrow a phrase from our friends the gourmets—even though we are more modest in our tastes—*à votre santé* (to your health) and to the happiness that health brings.

Antioxidant Equivalents

Vitamin C Measurements

1 ounce = approximately 7 teaspoons

Common Measures	Milligrams	Grams	Kilograms
1 pound	453,600	approx. 453 ½	approx. ½
approx. 2.2 pounds	1,000,000	1,000	1
1 teaspoon*	4,000	4	
¼ teaspoon	1,000	1	
1 ounce	28,350	approx. 28 ⅓	

*U.S. standard measuring spoon (the average dining room teaspoon).

Vitamin E Measurements
(D-alpha tocopheral equivalents)

Common Measures	Milligrams
1 IU (International Unit)	1 mg

Beta Carotene Measurements
(plant sources)

Common Measures	Micrograms
1 IU	1.16 mcg

5 IU = 1 Retinol Equivalent = 6 mcg beta carotene or 1 mcg from animal sources.

Weights and Measures

dash	=	2-4 drops				
3 teaspoons	=	1 tablespoon	=	½ fluid ounce	=	15 milliliters
4 tablespoons	=	¼ cup	=	2 fluid ounces	=	60 milliliters
16 tablespoons	=	1 cup (½ pint)	=	8 fluid ounces	=	240 milliliters
2 cups	=	1 pint	=	16 fluid ounces	=	480 milliliters
2 pints	=	1 quart	=	32 fluid ounces	=	960 milliliters
					=	0.96 liter
4 quarts	=	1 gallon	=	128 fluid ounces	=	3,840 milliliters
					=	3.8 liters
2 tablespoons	=	1 ounce	=	⅛ cup	=	30 grams
4 tablespoons	=	2 ounces	=	¼ cup	=	60 grams
16 tablespoons	=	8 ounces	=	1 cup	=	240 grams
2 cups	=	16 ounces	=	1 pound	=	480 grams
					=	0.48 kilogram

Appetizers

The main purpose of an appetizer is to stimulate the stomach for the main courses to come. There are a number of ways to do this. We once knew a chemical engineer so scientific in his whole lifestyle that his idea of an appetizer was to throw a few drops of hydrochloric acid into a beaker of water and down it, on the perfectly sound theory that this would give the acids of his stomach's gastric juices a head start on their work to come.

Well, we like to think that the appetizer course is a social nicety as well as a tooling-up course for your own stomach acids; but even with so modest a role as this, there are certain things to keep in mind.

First, the appetizer course should contrast with the entrées to be served later; that is, the canapés should not foreshadow tastes that are going to be major parts of the dinner ahead. Eliminate tomatoes from your canapé spreads if tomato sauce will be a feature of the coming meal; otherwise, the appetizer would spoil the later appreciation of the sauce. Second, if there's a heavy meal scheduled, large canapé spreads are going to take too much of an edge off the guests' appetites.

Finally, appetizers should be attractive and easy to handle.

VEGETABLE DIPPERS

SERVES 6
about 75 mg vitamin C per serving   •   ☆ Beta Carotene

1 cup sliced carrot	**2 cups broccoli florets**
2 tablespoons water	**1 cup fresh mushrooms**
2 cups cauliflower florets	**1 cup sliced cucumber**

Combine carrot slices and water in 1½-quart casserole; cover. Microwave on High (100%) 3-4 minutes or until just tender. Add cauliflower and broccoli; cover. Microwave on High 2-3 minutes or until just tender; stir once. Add mushrooms and cucumber. Microwave on High about 2 minutes.

Per Serving: 1-1¼ cups
Calories: 41
Fat: 0.3 gm
Cholesterol: 0 mg
Sodium: 36 mg
Carbohydrate: 7.1 gm
Protein: 2.2 gm

EASY RED PEPPER PESTO

MAKES 1 CUP
88 mg vitamin C per serving   •   ☆ Beta Carotene

2 (7 oz.) jars roasted	**½ teaspoon garlic powder**
red peppers	**½ teaspoon onion powder**
2-3 teaspoons chili powder	**½ teaspoon salt, if desired**

In strainer, drain red peppers well; pat dry with paper towels. In food processor fitted with metal wing blade, combine peppers, chili powder, garlic and onion powders, and salt; process until smooth (about 15 seconds). Spoon into serving dish. Serve with sliced raw vegetables or low-calorie crackers, if desired.

Per Serving: 2 tablespoons
Calories: 19
Fat: 0.4 gm
Cholesterol: 0 mg
Sodium: 148 mg
Carbohydrate: 3.2 gm
Protein: 0.4 gm

VEGETABLE MEDLEY

SERVES 8
170 mg vitamin C per serving • ☆ *Beta Carotene*

1 green pepper
1 sweet red pepper
6 carrots
2 cucumbers
6 white radishes

2 stalks celery
12 young green onions
1 recipe Curry Dip
(recipe below)

Trim, peel, and seed vegetables as necessary. Cut peppers, carrots, cucumbers, radishes, and celery into strips. Put in plastic bag; squeeze out air.
Seal and refrigerate at least 3 hours. Arrange all vegetables attractively on serving dish. Serve with Curry Dip (recipe below).

Per Serving: about 1 cup vegetables + 2-3 tablespoons dip
Calories: 96
Fat: 0.8 gm
Cholesterol: 2 mg
Sodium: 213 mg
Carbohydrate: 14.0 gm
Protein: 8.0 gm

CURRY DIP

MAKES 1½ CUPS
43 mg vitamin C per tablespoon

1 medium tomato, peeled
1½ teaspoon curry powder
1 green onion, sliced
¼ cup watercress leaves

8 ounces low-fat cottage
cheese
¼ teaspoon salt
¼ teaspoon "C"

Cut tomato into quarters. Place all ingredients in blender. Process on high speed until thoroughly blended (about 30 seconds). Stop blender occasionally to scrape down sides as necessary. Serve as a dip with cold raw vegetables.

Per Serving: 2-3 tablespoons
Calories: 29
Fat: 0.4 gm
Cholesterol: 2 mg
Sodium: 187 mg
Carbohydrate: 2.2 gm
Protein: 6.1 gm

SHANGHAI PARTY PLEASERS
MAKES 2 DOZEN
6 mg vitamin C per serving • ☆ *Beta Carotene* • ☆ *E*

1 can (20 oz.) crushed
   pineapple in juice, undrained
¼ cup firmly packed
   brown sugar
2 tablespoons cornstarch
1 teaspoon ginger
1 cup water
2 tablespoons margarine
1 pound finely chopped,
   cooked, skinned turkey
   or chicken

¾ cup oat-bran cereal,
   uncooked
⅓ cup plain low-fat yogurt
⅓ cup finely chopped
   water chestnuts, drained
⅓ cup sliced green onions
2 tablespoons low-salt
   soy sauce
1 egg white, slightly beaten
½ teaspoon salt, if desired

Preheat oven to 400° F.

Drain pineapple; reserve juice. In medium saucepan, combine brown sugar, cornstarch, and dash of ginger; mix well. Add pineapple juice, water, ¼ cup pineapple, and margarine; mix well. Bring to boil over medium-high heat; reduce heat. Simmer about 1 minute; stir frequently or until sauce is thickened and clear. Set aside.

Lightly coat rack of 13-x 9-inch baking pan with vegetable-oil cooking spray, or oil lightly. Combine turkey, oat bran, yogurt, water chestnuts, onions, soy sauce, egg white, salt, and remaining ginger and pineapple; mix well. Shape into 1-inch balls. Place on prepared rack.

Bake 20-25 minutes, or until light golden brown. Serve with sauce.

Note: Arrange these meatballs on a skewer with carrots, red and green peppers for increased vitamins A and C.

Per Serving: 2 appetizers
Calories: 161
Fat: 4.2 gm
Cholesterol: 29 mg
Sodium: 168 mg
Carbohydrate: 17.8 gm
Protein: 12.8 gm

SHRIMP COCKTAIL

SERVES 6
170 mg vitamin C per serving

3 quarts boiling water
2 tablespoons juice from lemon
1 teaspoon salt (optional)
½ teaspoon freshly ground pepper

1½ pounds raw shrimp
1 recipe Seafood Cocktail
 Sauce (below)

When water is boiling, add lemon juice, salt, pepper, and shrimp. Return water to boil. Cook 3-4 minutes, depending on size of shrimp. Remove from water at once. Rinse under cold water; shell and devein. Chill. Serve with cocktail sauce.

Per Serving: 3 oz. cooked shrimp and cocktail sauce made without salt
Calories: 177
Fat: 2 gm
Cholesterol: 173 mg
Sodium: 283 mg
Carbohydrate: 16.4 gm
Protein: 23.1 gm

SEAFOOD COCKTAIL SAUCE

SERVES 6 (APPROXIMATELY 1 CUP)
175 mg vitamin C per serving

1 cup low-sodium catsup
2 tablespoons lemon juice
¼ teaspoon hot pepper sauce

2 tablespoons prepared
 horseradish
¼ teaspoon "C"

Combine all ingredients and serve chilled.
This cocktail sauce makes a good accompaniment for raw clams, oysters, or cold cooked shrimp.

Per Serving: 2 tablespoons
Calories: 60
Fat: 0 gm
Cholesterol: 0 mg
Sodium: 114 mg
Carbohydrate: 14.8 gm
Protein: trace

SARDINE SPREAD

MAKES 1 CUP
248 mg vitamin C per serving • ☆ E

½ **medium onion, sliced**
3 tablespoons nonfat
  mayonnaise

1 (3½ oz.) can sardines
⅛ **teaspoon pepper**
¼ **teaspoon "C"**

Combine all ingredients in blender. Blend on high speed until smooth (about 20 seconds), stopping occasionally to push mixture into blades with rubber spatula as necessary.
Serve on thinly sliced bread or toast as appetizer, or use as sandwich filling.

Per Serving: 4 tablespoons
Calories: 70
Fat: 2.9 gm
Cholesterol: 36 mg
Sodium: 212 mg
Carbohydrate: 4.0 gm
Protein: 6.7 gm

GUACAMOLE

MAKES 2½ CUPS
104 mg vitamin C per serving

2 ripe avocados
2 tablespoons lime juice
½ **teaspoon "C"**
2 teaspoons grated onion
½ **teaspoon minced garlic**
¾ **teaspoon salt**

⅛ **teaspoon chili powder**
⅛ **teaspoon cumin**
Dash cayenne
⅓ **cup finely chopped,**
  peeled, seeded, ripe
  tomatoes

Peel avocados. Remove pit. Using fork, mash avocados with lime juice and "C." Stir in remaining ingredients and serve with tortilla chips.

Per Serving: 2 tablespoons
Calories: 18
Fat: 1.5 gm
Cholesterol: 0 mg
Sodium: 43 mg
Carbohydrate: 0.8 gm
Protein: 0.2 gm

BRAN-APPLE MUFFINS

MAKES 1 DOZEN
1 mg vitamin C per serving • ☆ E

**2 cups raw apples (2-3 medium-
  size apples), grated
  and firmly packed**
1 cup whole-wheat flour
½ cup millers bran
½ cup oat bran
½ cup old-fashioned rolled oats

1 tablespoon baking powder
½ cup skim milk
¼ cup corn oil
**½ cup raisins or date pieces
  or ¼ cup each**

Preheat oven to 375° F.
Cut apples in half; core and grate with raw side toward grater. Discard any
large pieces of peel. Combine dry ingredients and mix well. Add milk,
oil, apples, and raisins or dates and mix well again. Drop by spoonfuls
into oiled muffin pans. Bake 30 minutes or until toothpick inserted
into center of muffin comes out clean.

Per Serving: 1 muffin
Calories: 151
Fat: 5.3 gm
Cholesterol: trace
Sodium: 89 mg
Carbohydrate: 22.2 gm
Protein: 3.5 gm

OAT-BRAN PUFFS WITH CARROT FILLING

SERVES 8

5 mg vitamin C per serving • ☆ Beta Carotene • ☆ E

Shells:

1 cup low-fat milk
⅓ cup margarine
¾ cup all-purpose flour
¼ cup oat bran

Dash salt, if desired
4 eggs (or 1 cup egg substitute)

Filling:

5 medium carrots, sliced
1 tablespoon coarse horseradish
1 tablespoon chopped onion
¼ teaspoon celery salt or celery seed

2 tablespoons nonfat plain yogurt
2 tablespoons (low-fat brand) salad dressing

Preheat oven to 400° F.

Bring milk and margarine to boil in medium saucepan. Add flour, oat bran, and salt all at once. Stir quickly to form smooth paste that does not cling to side of pan; remove from heat. Add 1 egg at a time; beat vigorously after each one. Continue beating until eggs are combined. Place large table-spoons of dough onto baking sheet. Bake 10 minutes. Reduce heat to 350° F. and bake 25 minutes longer. Cool and cut horizontally to fill.

Place carrots in small saucepan and add enough water to cover. Cook until tender; drain well, reserving liquid. Combine 2 tablespoons cooking liquid with remaining ingredients. Spoon sauce over carrots and fill bran puffs.

Microwave tip: Combine carrots and ¼ cup water in 2-cup casserole; cover. Microwave on High 5-6 minutes or until tender. Continue as directed in recipe.

Per Serving: 1 puff
Calories: 209
Fat: 12.4 gm
Cholesterol: 109 mg
Sodium: 189 mg
Carbohydrate: 17.5 gm
Protein: 6.4 gm

FRUIT AND NUT NIBBLES

MAKES 8 CUPS
2 mg vitamin C per serving • ☆ *Beta Carotene* • ☆ *E*

4 cups old-fashioned rolled oats
1 cup coarsely chopped walnuts
½ cup sliced almonds
2 teaspoons ground cinnamon
¼ teaspoon ground ginger
⅛ teaspoon nutmeg
¼ cup safflower oil
¼ cup honey

2 tablespoons water
½ cup coarsely chopped dried apricots
½ cup coarsely chopped prunes
½ cup coarsely chopped dried apples
½ cup golden raisins

Preheat oven to 300° F. In large bowl, combine oats, walnuts, almonds, cinnamon, ginger, and nutmeg. Add oil, honey, and water; stir until moistened. Pour into a greased jelly-roll pan. Bake until golden (about 30 minutes), stirring occasionally. Set aside to cool. Stir in apricots, prunes, apples, and raisins.

Suggestions for gift-giving: Line an attractive tin with wax paper, add nibble mix, fold paper over to cover nibbles, and seal with lid. Wrap tin in clear cellophane paper, tie with a bow or length of narrow lace ribbon and add a thoughtful, written note on a tag. These could also be given in glass jars. (Nibbles should be refrigerated until you give them away—if they last that long!)

Per Serving: ½ cup
Calories: 262
Fat: 11.9 gm
Cholesterol: 0 mg
Sodium: 6.5 mg
Carbohydrate: 66.5 gm
Protein: 10.7 gm

VEGETABLE CREPES

SERVES 4
44 mg vitamin C per serving • ☆ Beta Carotene • ☆ E

8 (6") crepes
  (recipe below)
2 tablespoons margarine
2 cups thinly sliced carrots
  (about 3 medium)
½ cup sliced green onion
1 clove garlic, minced
  or pressed

2 cups thinly sliced
  zucchini (about 2 slender)
½ teaspoon dillweed
½ cup blanched slivered
  almonds, toasted
Pepper
Cheddar Sauce (recipe
  page 23)

Preheat oven to 350° F.
Prepare crepes; set aside. In large skillet, melt margarine. Add carrots, onion and garlic; sauté about 5 minutes. Stir in zucchini and dillweed; cover for 2-3 minutes. Add almonds; pepper to taste. Divide mixture among crepes; roll up and place on greased baking dish or oven-proof platter. Heat 5 minutes in oven or until crepes are hot. Pour Cheddar Sauce along center of crepes.

Per Serving: 2 crepes + ⅓ cup sauce
Calories: 423
Fat: 25.6 gm
Cholesterol: 75 mg
Sodium: 325 mg
Carbohydrate: 29.8 gm
Protein: 18.0 gm

CREPES

MAKES 16 CREPES
Trace vitamin C per serving

2 eggs
1 cup all-purpose flour

1¼ cups low-fat milk
1 tablespoon corn oil

In mixing bowl, lightly beat eggs. Gradually add flour alternately with milk, beating until smooth. Beat in corn oil, or combine ingredients in blender or food processor, and blend until smooth. Refrigerate batter at least 1 hour. Heat crepe pan and brush it once lightly with margarine. Take pan from heat; pour in 2-2½ tablespoons, or just enough batter to cover bottom, swirling pan to distribute batter evenly. Cook over medium-high heat about 1 minute or until edges loosen, top is dry, and underneath is golden. Invert crepe onto towel to cool. Repeat until all batter is used. Crepes may be stacked, wrapped in clean towel, placed in plastic bag and kept in refrigerator for 1-2 days. To freeze extra crepes, separate with wax paper; wrap well.

Per Serving: 2 plain crepes
Calories: 106
Fat: 3.5 gm
Cholesterol: 56 mg
Sodium: 35 mg
Carbohydrate: 13.9 gm
Protein: 4.5 gm

CHEDDAR SAUCE
MAKES 1¼-1½ CUPS
0.5 mg vitamin C per serving • ☆ Beta Carotene • ☆ E

1 tablespoon margarine
1 tablespoon all-purpose flour
¾ cup low-fat milk

**¾ cup (6 oz.) grated
low-fat cheddar**

In saucepan, melt margarine; add flour and cook, stirring constantly, over medium-low heat 2-3 minutes. Slowly stir in milk; continue stirring until sauce comes to boil. Reduce heat to low; add cheddar cheese. Stir until cheese is melted and sauce smooth.

Per Serving: about ⅓ cup
Calories: 116
Fat: 7.5 gm
Cholesterol: 19 mg
Sodium: 214 mg
Carbohydrate: 3.7 gm
Protein: 8.5 gm

Soups

The history of civilization may someday demand that the soup tureen be raised to its proper pedestal and lauded for helping children grow, strengthening the mature, nourishing the aged, sustaining the poor, and delighting the jaded palates of royalty.

Making good soup is an art, but an easy one to learn. Today's convenient, ready-made soups cannot compete with the soup we are talking about—the one on the back of the stove, which is the one true meal-in-itself of our cuisine.

Soups save money. They can be the main dish of a budget meal. They use leftovers and the less expensive cuts of meat. Most soups can be reheated to stretch your dollar further.

Use your imagination to decide how to serve soups—in bowls, mugs, wide-rimmed deep plates, tumblers, or cups. Whatever you use, take the time to chill the containers for cold soups and warm those for hot soups. This has a psychological as well as a physical effect.

Don't overlook the visual appeal. You will notice that many recipes in this section suggest a *garni*, or garnish. These have a physical basis, because they provide a contrast in taste or texture to the dish itself. Prepared with fresh, nutrient-rich vegetables, a bowl of soup provides a bounty of antioxidants, because the vitamins, leeched out by water during preparation, are retained in the broth.

In summary, though a soup may have its own taste appeal, its container—good to the touch and generous to the spirit—can enhance the taste and make the most modest and reliable plate of soup a high spot of the day.

BEEF BROTH

MAKES 5 QUARTS

About 200 mg vitamin C per serving • ☆ Beta Carotene

Get into the habit of saving leftover meat bones. When you visit your butcher, ask for some soup bones. Butchers used to give these away. Some still do, but as more and more people are becoming serious cost- and nutrition-conscious cooks, bones are not as easy to find. But for the small price, they are well worth it. If you don't have a cleaver, ask the butcher to crack the bones so that you get the full marrow in the broth. Wrap the bones and store in your freezer until ready to use.

1 pound beef bones	**4 stalks celery, coarsely**
2 pounds veal knuckles	**chopped**
3 pounds lean beef brisket	**1 clove garlic, mashed**
1 large onion studded with	**2 bay leaves**
4 cloves	**5½ quarts water**
½ cup fresh chopped parsley	**1 tablespoon salt (optional)**
4 leeks, carefully washed	**1 teaspoon "C"**
4 carrots, scrubbed and cut	
into 1" pieces	

Put all ingredients except salt and "C" in soup pot or large kettle, and bring to boil. As soup scum rises to surface, remove with skimmer or slotted spoon. Turn down heat and add salt. Cover and simmer for 2½ hours.
Strain, cool, and remove accumulated fat. Remove bay leaves from broth. Taste for seasoning, adding more salt if necessary. Add "C" and stir. Store in covered jars in refrigerator or freezer.

Per Serving: 1 cup
Calories: 27
Fat: 0.6 gm
Cholesterol: 5 mg
Sodium: 350 mg
Carbohydrate: 3.5 gm
Protein: 1.5 gm

VEGETABLE BROTH

MAKES 3 QUARTS
330 mg vitamin C per serving • ☆ Beta Carotene

In many vegetables, the highest concentration of nutrients is in and next to the skin, so it makes good sense to save the peelings.
Keep a plastic bag in the refrigerator for unused peelings from potatoes, carrots, and other vegetables. Scrub the vegetables lightly with a brush. Dry and peel.
Also save tops of carrots, turnips, beet greens, pea shells, green pepper stems, outer leaves of lettuce and cabbage. Always squeeze as much air as possible out of the bag before closing. Store in freezer until ready to use.

**Contents of plastic bag (above),
  plus 1 large onion, coarsely
  chopped *or***
**4 leeks, carefully washed
  and chopped**
**2 carrots, scrubbed and
  coarsely chopped**
**5 stalks celery, including tops,
  coarsely chopped**
½ cup fresh parsley

1 bay leaf
1 clove garlic, mashed
3½ quarts water
1 teaspoon "C"
1 tablespoon salt (optional)
1 teaspoon pepper

Place all ingredients, except "C," salt, and pepper, in stock pot or large kettle. Bring to boil; reduce heat. Cover and simmer for 1 hour and 30 minutes. Season to taste with salt and pepper. Strain. Remove bay leaves from broth. Cool and add "C."
If not using broth immediately, it may be stored in the refrigerator or freezer.
This broth may be served by itself or used as a base for other soups.

Per Serving: 1 cup with salt added
Calories: 20
Fat: 0.1 gm
Cholesterol: 0 mg
Sodium: 666 mg
Carbohydrate: 4.0 gm
Protein: 0.7 gm

CHICKEN BROTH

MAKES 5 QUARTS
About 200 mg vitamin C per serving • ☆ Beta Carotene

1 (4-5 lbs.) chicken
1 veal knuckle
6 leeks, carefully washed
   and chopped
4 carrots, scrubbed and cut
   into 1" pieces
2 stalks celery, including
   tops, coarsely chopped

1 medium onion, studded
   with 4 cloves
1 bay leaf
¼ teaspoon thyme
5½ quarts water
1 tablespoon salt (optional)
1 teaspoon "C"

Place all ingredients except salt and "C" in a stock pot or large kettle. Bring to boil. As liquid heats, scum will rise to surface. Remove frequently with skimmer or slotted spoon. Reduce heat. Cover and simmer for 2 hours and 30 minutes.

Correct seasoning with salt. Strain through fine sieve. Remove bay leaf. Refrigerate to cool. Add "C" and stir thoroughly. When fat has solidified on top of broth, discard it. Store (see Beef Broth for instructions).

Per Serving: 1 cup
Calories: 25
Fat: 0.3 gm
Cholesterol: 3 mg
Sodium: 352 mg
Carbohydrate: 3.8 gm
Protein: 1.5 gm

CREAM OF TOMATO SOUP

SERVES 6
200 mg vitamin C per serving • ☆ *Beta Carotene*

**2 pounds ripe or 4 cups
  canned tomatoes
1 medium onion, chopped
¼ teaspoon celery seed
3 tablespoons tomato paste
1 bay leaf
2 whole cloves
1½ cups skim milk**

**½ cup evaporated skim milk
¼ cup corn oil margarine
¼ cup flour
½ teaspoon salt
¼ teaspoon freshly ground
  pepper
¼ teaspoon "C"
Chopped fresh parsley**

Peel, core, and seed tomatoes. Simmer tomatoes, onion, celery seed,
tomato paste, bay leaf, and cloves in large saucepan for 15 minutes, until
tomatoes are tender.
While tomatoes are cooking, heat milk and evaporated milk until hot. Melt
margarine in saucepan. When it begins to bubble, remove pan from heat
and stir in flour. When thoroughly mixed, return to heat and add hot milk.
Stir constantly until white sauce has thickened. Season with salt and pepper.
Press tomatoes and onion through sieve. There should be about 2 cups of
purée. Add tomato purée to white sauce while stirring. Remove bay leaf. Stir
in "C." Serve hot or cold. If you are serving soup cold, add "C" just before
serving. Garnish with chopped parsley, if desired.

*Per Serving: about 1½ cups
Calories: 179
Fat: 8.0 gm
Cholesterol: 2 mg
Sodium: 367 mg
Carbohydrate: 19.9 gm
Protein: 6.4 gm*

CARROT SOUP

SERVES 5
43 mg vitamin C per serving • ☆ *Beta Carotene* • ☆ *E*

2 cups carrots, grated
1 cup Chicken Broth (recipe
  page 28)
1 cup light cream

1 tablespoon honey
½ small onion, diced
½ teaspoon nutmeg
½ teaspoon cinnamon

In large saucepan, combine carrots, broth, and cream. Mix well. Stir in honey, adding onion and seasonings. Cook over medium heat, stirring frequently.
Serve in individual soup bowls and sprinkle with nutmeg and cinnamon.

Per Serving: ¾ cup
Calories: 139
Fat: 9.5 gm
Cholesterol: 33 mg
Sodium: 146 mg
Carbohydrate: 11.0 gm
Protein: 2.2 gm

CARROT-POTATO SOUP

SERVES 6
19 mg vitamin C per serving • ☆ *Beta Carotene*

1 tablespoon canola oil
¾ cup chopped onion
2 cans (12 oz.) carrot juice
1¾ cups potatoes, peeled, diced
¼ teaspoon salt (optional)
¼ teaspoon ground mace

1/16 teaspoon ground
  black pepper
1 cup skim milk
¼ cup plain low-fat yogurt
Raw carrot, grated

In medium saucepan, heat canola oil until hot. Add onion; sauté until transparent, about 5 minutes. Add carrot juice, potatoes, salt, mace, and black pepper. Bring to boil. Reduce heat and simmer, covered, until potatoes are tender, about 8 minutes. Remove from heat. Pour half of hot mixture into container of electric blender. Process until smooth, stopping to scrape down sides. Transfer to bowl and repeat with remaining mixture. Return all to saucepan; add milk. Heat until hot. Serve each portion topped with 1 tablespoon yogurt and sprinkle of grated carrot, if desired.

Per Serving: ⅔ cup
Calories: 139
Fat: 2.8 grams
Cholesterol: 2 mg
Sodium: 161 mg
Carbohydrate: 23.9 gm
Protein: 4.3 gm

CREAM OF BROCCOLI SOUP

SERVES 6
216 mg vitamin C per serving • ☆ *Beta Carotene*

1 medium onion, sliced
1 clove garlic, peeled
1 medium carrot, sliced
1 stalk celery, coarsely chopped
2 cups broccoli, coarsely chopped
½ cup water
1 teaspoon salt (optional)

Dash cayenne
½ cup cooked macaroni, spaghetti, or other pasta
¼ teaspoon "C"
1 cup Chicken Broth (recipe page 28)
½ cup evaporated skim milk

Place vegetables and garlic in water; simmer for 10 minutes or until tender. Place in blender. Add salt, cayenne, pasta, and "C." Process on high, adding broth and cream gradually until smooth.
Serve hot by heating over simmering water (or in a double boiler), or serve cold with spoonful of nonfat sour cream.

Per Serving: ¾-1 cup with salt added
Calories: 69
Fat: 0.5 gm
Cholesterol: 6 mg
Sodium: 469 mg
Carbohydrate: 11.9 gm
Protein: 3.9 gm

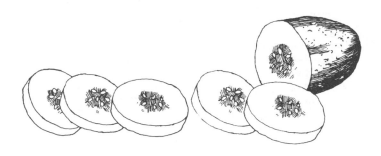

COLD CREAM-OF-CUCUMBER SOUP

SERVES 6
160 mg vitamin C per serving

**1½ pounds or 3 large, 8"
cucumbers, peeled and seeded**
3 tablespoons margarine
**½ cup minced shallots or
scallions or onions or
combination of all three**
**6 cups Chicken Broth
(recipe page 28)**
½ teaspoon white wine vinegar
**¾ teaspoon dried tarragon (or
1 tablespoon fresh dillweed)**

**4 tablespoons uncooked
Cream of Wheat (quick-
cooking)**
½ teaspoon salt (optional)
¼ teaspoon pepper
1 cup nonfat sour cream
¼ teaspoon "C"
**2 tablespoons fresh parsley,
minced**

Cut half of 1 cucumber into paper-thin slices and reserve for garnish.
Cut remaining cucumbers into ½-inch pieces—about 4½ cups.
Melt margarine in 4-quart saucepan. Cook shallots, scallions, and/or onions slowly in margarine until tender and transparent, but not brown.
Add cucumber pieces, Chicken Broth, wine vinegar, and tarragon or dillweed. Bring soup to boil and add Cream of Wheat, stirring slightly. Simmer partially covered for 20 minutes.
Purée soup in blender until smooth and return soup to pan. Add more Chicken Broth if soup is too thick. Season with salt and pepper. Add salt, as anything served chilled needs more salt than when it is served hot.
Bring soup to a simmer and add ½ cup sour cream, mixing well.
Remove from heat.
Cool to room temperature, uncovered. Stir in "C," cover, and chill.
Ladle into chilled soup bowls and garnish with spoonful of nonfat sour cream, cucumber slices, and minced parsley.
To serve this same soup hot: After you have added sour cream to simmering soup, stir in "C" and serve in warm soup bowls. Garnish with sour cream, cucumber slices, and parsley, as with cold soup.

Per Serving: about 1½-2 cups each
Calories: 175
Fat: 0.5 gm
Cholesterol: 3 mg
Sodium: 649 mg
Carbohydrate: 23.0 gm
Protein: 6.5 gm

CREAM OF BRUSSELS SPROUTS SOUP

SERVES 8
210 mg vitamin C per serving

4 pieces fresh bacon, diced
1½ pounds Brussels sprouts
  coarsely chopped, or
2 packages (10 oz.) frozen
  Brussels sprouts, thawed
1 medium onion
2 cups Chicken Broth
  (recipe page 28)

½ teaspoon salt
½ teaspoon freshly
  ground pepper
¼ teaspoon thyme
¼ teaspoon basil
½ cup evaporated skim milk
¼ teaspoon "C"

Cook diced bacon until crisp. Remove and drain on paper towels. Simmer crisp bacon and Brussels sprouts, onion, Chicken Broth, salt, pepper, thyme, and basil in saucepan for 15 minutes or until sprouts are tender. Place half of mixture in a blender and process on high speed until smooth. Blend remaining half into processor. Return mixture to saucepan and add evaporated skim milk and "C." Taste for seasoning. Heat thoroughly.

Per Serving: about 1 cup
Calories: 122
Fat: 1.7 gm
Cholesterol: 4 mg
Sodium: 329 mg
Carbohydrate: 11.7 gm
Protein: 7.0 gm

MUSHROOM BISQUE
SERVES 6
170 mg vitamin C per serving

1 pound fresh mushrooms
4 cups Chicken Broth
(recipe page 28)
4 tablespoons corn oil
margarine
3 tablespoons flour
¼ teaspoon dry mustard

¼ teaspoon pepper
¼ cup dry sherry
½ cup evaporated skim
milk
¼ teaspoon "C"
¼ teaspoon paprika

Wipe mushrooms with damp cloth to remove dirt particles. Remove stems and chop finely. Set caps aside. Mix chopped stems and Chicken Broth in saucepan and simmer for 30 minutes. Strain and discard stems.
Melt margarine in skillet and sauté mushroom caps until lightly browned. Sprinkle in flour and mustard. When well blended, gradually add Chicken Broth and continue stirring until mixture thickens. Cook over lowest possible heat for 10 minutes, stirring occasionally. Add salt and pepper to taste and stir in sherry and skim milk. Cook 2 minutes and stir in "C." Serve with paprika sprinkled on top.

Per Serving: about 1 cup
Calories: 159
Fat: 8.2 gm
Cholesterol: 3 mg
Sodium: 334 mg
Carbohydrate: 13.8 gm
Protein: 4.5 gm

GREEK LEMON SOUP

SERVES 6
170 mg vitamin C per serving

**6 cups Chicken Broth (recipe
  page 28) or use canned
6 tablespoons raw rice
1 cup egg substitute
3 tablespoons strained fresh
  lemon juice**

**Pinch freshly ground
  white pepper
¼ teaspoon "C"
2 tablespoons fresh parsley,
  finely chopped**

Note: If you use canned broth, refrigerate can overnight. Any fat will rise to surface and solidify, making it easy to remove.

Place Chicken Broth in 3- to 4-quart enamel or stainless steel saucepan and bring to rapid boil.

Add rice. Stir once or twice and turn heat down to low. Partially cover pan and simmer rice for 20 minutes or until soft.

Using wire whisk or hand mixer, beat eggs in bowl until foamy (but do not overbeat) and stir in lemon juice. One tablespoon at a time, stir 4 table-spoons of warm broth into egg and lemon mixture. Add remaining warm broth and rice in a slow, steady stream. Return soup to saucepan over low heat and stir constantly for 3 minutes or until mixture reaches consistency of custard. Never let soup come to boil, or eggs will curdle.

(If soup should curdle, and it can happen to the best of cooks, you can strain it through a fine sieve into another saucepan, beating constantly with wire whisk. Clean any remaining egg off rice by running rice under hot water and return to soup. Your soup will be thinner than usual, but certainly all right to serve.)

Taste soup for seasoning. Add pepper and salt to taste. Add "C."

Sprinkle with finely chopped parsley and serve at once in warm bowls.

Note: This soup can be made in advance and refrigerated. Be careful when reheating that you do not allow it to boil, or it will curdle. Add parsley just before serving.

Per Serving: about 1 cup
Calories: 67
Fat: 0.3 gm
Cholesterol: 3 mg
Sodium: 407 mg
Carbohydrate: 10.1 gm
Protein: 5.4 gm

GAZPACHO
SERVES 4
323 mg vitamin C per serving • ☆ Beta Carotene • ☆ E

1 clove garlic, peeled
1 Spanish onion, peeled,
   and sliced
1 cucumber, peeled, seeded,
   and sliced
1 green pepper, seeded,
   and sliced
3 ripe tomatoes, quartered

1 cup spiced vegetable juice,
   clam and tomato juice, or
   tomato juice
¼ teaspoon salt
¼ teaspoon pepper
¼ teaspoon "C"
2 tablespoons corn oil
1 tablespoon red wine
   vinegar

Combine all ingredients into blender and process until last bit of pepper and cucumber is cut up.
Chill and pour into cold mugs or bowls. Serve with garnish (below) and croutons, if desired.

Garnish
2 tablespoons green pepper,
   finely chopped
2 tablespoons cucumber, peeled,
   seeded, and finely chopped

2 tablespoons scallions,
   thinly sliced

Per Serving: 1½ cups
Calories: 133
Fat: 7.3 gm
Cholesterol: 0 mg
Sodium: 312 mg
Carbohydrate:14.0 gm
Protein: 2.3 gm

GARLIC CROUTONS
SERVES 8
Trace vitamin C in each serving • ☆ E

2 cups ½" cubes whole
   grain bread, crusts removed
½ cup oil (corn or safflower)

1 teaspoon garlic,
   finely chopped

Note: The best croutons are made from 2-day-old French or Italian bread, but plain white bread will be all right if that's all you have.

If you are using fresh bread, cut into slices and spread them out on baking tray; put in oven at 200° F for about 10 minutes to dry out. Remove crust and cut bread into ½-inch cubes. Cover bottom of large, heavy frying pan with thin layer of oil (⅛ inch) and heat almost to smoking. Drop in bread cubes and toss with wooden spoons until croutons begin to brown. Add a little more oil if needed. Turn off heat and add garlic. It will cook by the heat of pan. The important thing to remember is to add garlic just before bread is done; garlic pieces will adhere to bread. Drain on paper towels and cool before serving.

Per Serving: 1½ tablespoons
Calories: 100
Fat: 7.3 gm
Cholesterol: 0 mg
Sodium: 80 mg
Carbohydrate: 6.9 gm
Protein: 1.5 gm

GARDEN SOUP

SERVES 8
25 mg vitamin C per serving • ☆ Beta Carotene

1 **medium onion, chopped**
1 **tablespoon low-fat margarine**
3 **medium potatoes, peeled and diced**
4 **medium carrots, peeled and sliced**
1 **medium stalk celery, sliced**

2 **tablespoons parsley, chopped**
3 **chicken bouillon cubes (low sodium optional)**
⅛ **teaspoon pepper**
5 **cups water**

In large, heavy, nonstick kettle or Dutch oven, cook onion in margarine. Add remaining ingredients and 5 cups water. Cover and simmer 40 minutes or until vegetables are tender. Serve as is, or purée in an electric blender and reheat.

Per Serving: 1-1¼ cups
Calories: 93
Fat: 0.8 gm
Cholesterol: 0 mg
Sodium: 371 mg
Carbohydrate: 18.7 gm
Protein: 2.2 gm

SPINACH AND TURNIP SOUP
SERVES 6
211 mg vitamin C per serving   •   ☆ Beta Carotene

**1½ pounds fresh white
turnips, peeled, cut into
thin slices**
3 tablespoons margarine
1¼ teaspoons sugar
**4 cups tightly packed fresh
turnip greens and fresh
spinach or tightly packed
fresh spinach**

**4 cups Chicken Broth
(recipe page 28) (or use
2 cups canned stock,
2 cups water)**
**3 tablespoons uncooked
Cream of Wheat
(quick-cooking)**
¼ teaspoon "C"
1½ cups warm skim milk

Slowly cook turnips in 2 tablespoons margarine and 1 teaspoon sugar, over low heat, until tender (about 10 minutes). Set aside.

While turnips are cooking, clean greens and spinach. Drain and pat dry with towels. Melt 1 tablespoon margarine in large skillet, enamel or Teflon. When margarine begins to bubble, add greens and spinach. Toss with wooden spoons. Add remaining ¼ teaspoon sugar and salt, if desired. Cook until greens have become limp and tender, about 3 to 4 minutes. Place cooked turnips, spinach, and greens in blender. Add 1 cup Chicken Broth and purée. Pour puréed mixture into 5- or 6-quart saucepan. Add remaining Chicken Broth. Sprinkle in Cream of Wheat and simmer for 5 minutes, stirring occasionally. Add "C" and milk. Taste for seasoning. Heat thoroughly.

Per Serving: 1½-2 cups
Calories: 144
Fat: 6.2 gm
Cholesterol: 3 mg
Sodium: 376 mg
Carbohydrate: 16.3 gm
Protein: 5.4 gm

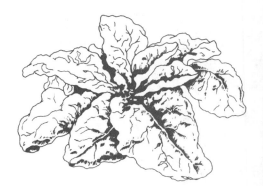

FISH SOUP SAINT TROPEZ

SERVES 6
88 mg vitamin C per serving   •   ☆ Beta Carotene   •   ☆ E

1 tablespoon olive oil
2 medium onions, chopped
2 carrots, peeled and chopped
2 green peppers (better yet,
   1 green and 1 red)
2 cloves garlic, minced
1 can (28 oz.) whole
   peeled tomatoes
1 bay leaf
½ teaspoon dried red-pepper
   flakes, crushed
3 strips orange peel, each
   about ½" x 3"
½ teaspoon fennel seeds

½ teaspoon thyme
3 medium potatoes, peeled
   and cut in ½" cubes
3 cups water
1 cup dry vermouth or
   white wine
2 pounds fresh or frozen
   fish (snapper, cod, bass,
   blackfish, or halibut),
   partially thawed, if
   frozen, and cut in chunks
½ cup minced fresh parsley
¼ teaspoon salt
¼ teaspoon pepper

Heat oil in large pot or kettle and sauté onions, carrots, peppers, and garlic in hot oil until tender. Add tomatoes, bay leaf, crushed red pepper, orange peel, fennel seeds, thyme, and potatoes. Cover and simmer 10 minutes. Add water and vermouth, and bring to boil. Reduce heat and simmer uncovered 5 minutes. Add fish and parsley and cook 2-5 minutes or until fish flakes easily (don't overcook). Remove orange peel and bay leaf. Season to taste with salt and pepper; serve warm in bowls.

Per Serving: about 1½ cups
Calories: 323
Fat: 3.6 gm
Cholesterol: 65 mg
Sodium: 262 mg
Carbohydrate: 28.9 gm
Protein: 29.0 gm

VEGETABLE SOUP

SERVES 6
240 mg vitamin C per serving   •   ☆ Beta Carotene

**4 cups Vegetable Broth
(recipe page 27)**
**1 cup cut-up string beans
(1" pieces)**
**3 medium carrots, scrubbed,
peeled, and very thinly sliced**

1 cup green peas
2 stalks celery, thinly sliced
½ onion, finely chopped
2 tablespoons margarine
½ sweet red pepper, chopped
¼ teaspoon pepper

Bring Vegetable Broth to a boil and add string beans, carrots, green peas, and celery. Reduce heat and simmer 5 minutes.

While vegetables are cooking, sauté onions in margarine.

When vegetables have simmered 5 minutes, add red pepper and cook another 10 minutes, or until vegetables are just tender. Add onion and margarine. Season with salt and pepper to taste.

Per Serving: 1¼-1½ cups
Calories: 101
Fat: 4.0 gm
Cholesterol: 0 mg
Sodium: 504 mg
Carbohydrate: 13.2 gm
Protein: 2.8 gm

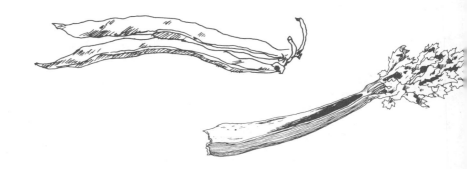

ROOTS AND TUBERS SOUP

SERVES 8-10
230 mg vitamin C per serving • ☆ *Beta Carotene*

**8 cups Chicken Broth
(recipe page 28)**
**1 can (14½ oz.) stewed
tomatoes**
1 can (6 oz.) tomato paste
1 medium onion, chopped
1 carrot, sliced
**1 small turnip, peeled and
cubed**

1 parsnip, peeled and sliced
2 stalks celery, sliced
**2 medium potatoes (about
⅔ pound), cubed**
**1½ cup chopped green
cabbage**
2 bay leaves
1½ teaspoons ground sage
½ teaspoon black pepper

In 6-quart pot, combine all ingredients; bring to boil. Cover, reduce heat, and simmer about 25-30 minutes or until vegetables are tender. Remove bay leaves. Serve hot. Soup can be stored, covered, in refrigerator up to 1 week.

Per Serving: about 1 cup
Calories: 117
Fat: 1 gm
Cholesterol: 2 mg
Sodium: 1370 mg*
Carbohydrates: 23.1 gm
Protein: 3.5gm

**For those on sodium-restricted diets, use low-sodium Chicken Broth.
Sodium value per serving: 368 mg*

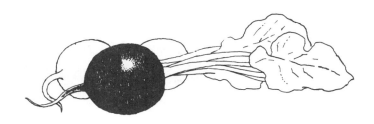

Mr. Davies,

12/5
5:30pm

Dr Cory SerVaas sent me over here to talk to you about high temperature cooking of meats & fats

Please call me at 636-8881 ext 315

Christina Ferroli, Ph.D.

Meat, Chicken, & Fish

Why add vitamin C to a processed meat dish or the salad beside it? For starters (with the exception of liver), there is hardly any natural vitamin C in meat, poultry, or fish. A more important reason, however, is that meat packers and processors add nitrates to processed, smoked, or cured meats to keep them from spoiling. But nitrates break down to form dangerous nitrosamines, known to be carcinogenic in animals and believed to be carcinogenic in human beings. To counteract that problem, packers then add vitamin C to the meat to delay the formation of nitrosamines. But vitamin C isn't as stable as nitrosamines, even in the best of conditions. Consequently, we suggest you include additional vitamin C in any recipe that includes processed meats.

These include ham, bacon, pastrami, bologna, corned beef, dried beef, pickle loaf, sausages, hot dogs, and other lunch meats. Sixty-five to seventy percent of all pork products in the United States are cured. Our recipes include only fresh meats, but we must be realists. If your family enjoys cured and smoked meat dishes, we suggest that you add one-half teaspoon of vitamin C per six servings of these dishes. Vitamin C can be conveniently added to ham casseroles, chipped beef on toast, beans and franks, and any number of processed meat recipes.

In addition to alleviating the dangerous effects of nitrates in processed meat, vitamin C performs as a good substitute for the nitrates in preventing discoloration of the meat. Even though nitrates are under serious scrutiny by the F.D.A. and the U.S.D.A., no practical substitute has as yet been found to prevent spoilage and extend shelf life of processed meats.

We believe it is prudent to use only fresh meats whenever possible.

Since meat is such a familiar protein staple on the family dinner table, we have made a special effort to find recipes that may be improved by the addition of vitamin C in their preparation.

There have been libraries of books written advising the shopper how to select proper meat cuts without incurring unnecessary expense. Probably the most sensible answer to the problem is to find a good reliable butcher, if you are so lucky as to live in a neighborhood where the small retailer holds forth.

It is now recommended by the National Livestock and Meat Board that meat be cooked to an internal temperature of 140° F or greater to prevent bacterial contamination and illness.

We recommend a meat thermometer for better cooking control. It is the only way you can be sure of the state of doneness.

Generally speaking, avoid high cooking temperatures except for a final flourish to crisp roasts or broiled meats, since excessive heat tends to extract the juices from the meat. Salt does the same thing. Salt just before serving, if it is needed. Only in recipes such as stews, where you wish to draw some of the meat juices into the liquid, should you salt during cooking.

A word about poultry. If you can, buy fresh poultry. It will be far superior to that which has been frozen. If you are cooking chicken in pieces, the white meat will require less cooking time than the dark, so it should be added later.

On fish: Fish is cooked very quickly, until just before the flesh begins to flake, at about 150 degrees F. It may be broiled, fried (if breaded), baked, or poached. Perfectly cooked fish is firm to the touch, yet juicy.

For the adventurous, we've included a recipe for Seviche, a method of "cooking" fish in citrus juice and vitamin C powder.

STUFFED WHOLE SAVOY CABBAGE

SERVES 6
90 mg vitamin C per serving • ☆ *Beta Carotene*

1 large Savoy cabbage
1 pound very lean
  ground beef
¾ pound ground lean pork
5 shallots, finely minced
2 cloves garlic, finely minced
¼ cup fresh parsley,
  finely chopped
½ teaspoon salt
¼ teaspoon freshly
  ground pepper
2 tablespoons corn
  oil margarine

1 large onion, finely
  chopped
4 large carrots, thinly sliced
1 cup Beef Broth (recipe
  page 26) or may substitute
  low-sodium variety
1 bay leaf
¼ teaspoon thyme
1 cup Tomato Sauce
  (recipe page 47)

Discard any wilted or yellowed leaves from cabbage and wash remaining portion carefully. Place whole cabbage on rack over sink and pour large pan of boiling water over it. This will help separate leaves without damaging or detaching them. Drain cabbage.

Blend beef, pork, shallots, garlic, parsley, salt, and pepper together thoroughly. Carefully place meat stuffing in between cabbage leaves. When all stuffing has been used, close cabbage carefully and tie it firmly with a string. Heat margarine in saucepan large enough for cabbage. Add onion and carrots. Place cabbage on vegetables and add Beef Broth, bay leaf, and thyme. Cover pan tightly and place it over low heat. Simmer cabbage for 2 hours and 30 minutes, or until meat is tender. Remove bay leaf. Remove from pan and serve with tomato sauce.

Per Serving: 1½-2 cups
Calories: 299
Fat: 11.3 gm
Cholesterol: 77 mg
Sodium: 422 mg
Carbohydrate: 18.8 gm
Protein: 29.6 gm

GROUND BEEF WITH EGGPLANT

SERVES 6
225 mg vitamin C per serving • ☆ E

**1 medium eggplant, cut into
  1" cubes**
¼ cup corn or safflower oil
**1½ pounds very lean
  ground beef**
**2 tablespoons onion, finely
  minced**
**1 clove garlic, peeled and
  finely minced**

**2 tablespoons fresh parsley,
  finely chopped**
¼ teaspoon salt
¼ teaspoon pepper
¹⁄₁₆ teaspoon nutmeg
¹⁄₁₆ teaspoon marjoram
**1 cup Tomato Sauce
  (recipe page 47)**
¼ teaspoon "C"

Preheat oven to 350° F.
Fry eggplant cubes in oil 5 minutes, or until tender. Stir frequently with wooden spoon. Mix beef, onion, garlic, and parsley together. Season with salt, pepper, nutmeg, and marjoram. Place layer of beef in bottom of well-oiled casserole dish. Cover meat with layer of eggplant and add a little to-mato sauce. Continue layering until all beef and eggplant have been added. Pour remaining tomato sauce over top and bake for 40-45 minutes. Just be-fore removing beef from oven, sprinkle "C" over top to dissolve in cooking liquid. Serve very hot.

Per Serving: about 1 cup
Calories: 285
Fat: 15.9 gm
Cholesterol: 55 mg
Sodium: 348 mg
Carbohydrate: 11.5 gm
Protein: 23.2 gm

TOMATO SAUCE
SERVES 4 (2 CUPS)
275 mg vitamin C per serving

2 tablespoons olive oil
½ onion, coarsely chopped
2 cloves garlic, finely minced
1 pound tomatoes, peeled
1 green pepper, coarsely chopped
1 tablespoon tomato paste

2 tablespoons dry red wine (optional)
1 bay leaf
¼ cup fresh parsley leaves
½ teaspoon oregano
½ teaspoon basil
¼ teaspoon "C"

Heat oil in deep skillet over medium heat. Add onion and garlic.
Sauté, stirring frequently, until onion is translucent and golden. Transfer to blender.
Combine all ingredients, except "C," in blender. Process on high speed until smooth. Pour mixture back into skillet, simmering gently for 30 minutes. Remove bay leaf.
Stir in "C." Serve with pasta and freshly grated Parmesan cheese, or use in recipe.

Per Serving: ½ cup
Calories: 123
Fat: 7.5 gm
Cholesterol: 0 mg
Sodium: 40 mg
Carbohydrate: 10.2 gm
Protein: 2.2 gm

HUNGARIAN STUFFED CABBAGE

SERVES 4
24 mg vitamin C per serving • ☆ E

**1 head cabbage (preferably
  Savoy)**
**3 tablespoons corn
  oil margarine**
½ cup chopped onion
2 cups lamb, minced, cooked
3 tablespoons flour

1½ cups low-fat milk
**½ cup grated sharp low-
  fat cheddar cheese**
¼ teaspoon pepper
**¼ teaspoon Hungarian
  paprika**

Preheat oven to 350° F.
Remove outer leaves and hollow-out center of cabbage, leaving a cavity big enough for stuffing. Place in pan of boiling salted water. Cook 10 minutes. Drain in colander; squeeze out excess water.
Heat 1 tablespoon margarine in small skillet and sauté onion until golden brown. Mix with minced lamb.
Heat remaining margarine in small saucepan and stir in flour. Cook stirring constantly over low heat 2 minutes. Add milk and stir until mixture boils. Add cheese and continue stirring until cheese melts. Season with pepper. Add ½ cup mixture to lamb. Place cabbage, cavity side up, in small deep casserole so that sides will support cabbage. Fill cavity with meat mixture. Cover with cheese sauce and sprinkle with paprika. Bake 30 minutes.

Per Serving: ¼ stuffed cabbage
Calories: 382
Fat: 24.2 gm
Cholesterol: 74 mg
Sodium: 307 mg
Carbohydrate: 16.3 gm
Protein: 24.5 gm

BURMESE SHRIMP AND CABBAGE

SERVES 4

58 mg vitamin C per serving • ☆ E

**3 tablespoons canola or
sunflower oil**
2-3 cloves garlic, minced
**1½ pounds raw shrimp,
shelled**
**1 cup liquid drained from
canned tomatoes**
3-4 cups shredded cabbage

1 medium onion, chopped
**1 cup chopped canned
low-sodium tomatoes,
drained**
**2 tablespoons low-sodium
soy sauce**
**2 cups cooked rice
(prepared without salt)**

Heat oil with garlic in skillet over medium heat. Add shrimp and cook. Stir frequently, just until shrimp are pink. Remove from heat and set aside.
In large saucepan, bring tomato liquid to boil. Add cabbage and onion. Cover and reduce heat to simmer. Cook just until vegetables are tender. Add tomatoes. Just before serving, stir in shrimp and soy sauce. Serve over hot cooked rice.

Per Serving: ½ cup rice + 1½-2 cups sauce
Calories: 409
Fat: 13.6 gm
Cholesterol: 217 mg
Sodium: 404 mg
Carbohydrate: 37.1 gm
Protein: 34.2 gm

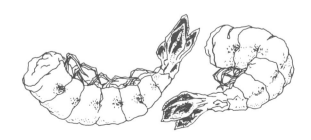

STUFFED PEPPERS

SERVES 6
220 mg vitamin C per serving

3 cups white bread cubes about
   ¾" square
3 cloves garlic, minced
6 anchovy fillets, chopped
¼ cup chopped fresh parsley
   (preferably flat leaf)
2 tablespoons capers
3 tablespoons currants
½ cup chopped ripe
   black olives

½ cup olive oil divided
   (for those on a fat-
   restricted diet, use
   ½ cup Beef Broth,
   recipe page 26)
3 large (or 6 small) sweet
   green or red peppers,
   cut in half
¼ teaspoon "C"

Preheat oven to 350° F.
Bread should be slightly stale. If very fresh, put cubes on baking sheet in medium oven until they dry out.
Combine bread cubes, garlic, anchovy fillets, parsley, capers, currants, olives, ¼ cup olive oil, and salt and pepper to taste. Toss them together lightly in mixing bowl.
If using small peppers, cut off tops. Remove stems and seeds and fill with stuffing. Do not pack down because stuffing will expand when baked. Dribble remaining oil evenly on peppers.
Bake in oven 45 minutes. Let cool to room temperature. Sprinkle on "C," and serve.
This makes a satisfying first course or accompaniment to fish, particularly in the summer.

Per Serving: ½ large or 1 small stuffed pepper
Calories: 335
Fat: 22.5 gm
Cholesterol: 2 mg
Sodium: 551 mg
Carbohydrate: 27.1 gm
Protein: 5.9 gm

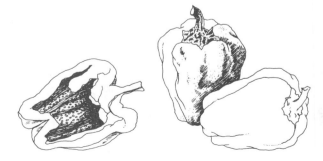

LAMB STEW

SERVES 6
200 mg vitamin C per serving ☆ *Beta Carotene*

2 tablespoons corn
  oil margarine
1 medium onion, thinly sliced
1 teaspoon paprika
2 pounds boneless lean
  lamb stew meat (shoulder
  or neck), cut into small
  serving pieces
1 cup Beef Broth
  (recipe page 26)
1 cup tomato purée
4 whole cloves
*Bouquet garni

5 medium potatoes, peeled
  and quartered
1 package (10 oz.)
  frozen peas
¼ pound mushrooms,
  sliced
4 medium carrots, chopped
Flour (as needed)
¼ teaspoon salt (optional)
¼ teaspoon pepper
1 cup nonfat sour cream
¼ teaspoon "C"
Chopped fresh parsley

Melt margarine in skillet over medium heat. Add onion and, stirring constantly, sauté until golden. Sprinkle with paprika, continuing to stir until blended.

Add meat, stirring frequently until browned. Remove lamb and onions to a stewpot or casserole with lid.

Add Beef Broth and tomato purée to margarine remaining in skillet. Blend thoroughly. Pour mixture over meat and onions.

Add cloves, bouquet garni, and potatoes. Bring to boil 1 minute. Reduce heat until liquid barely simmers. Cover and continue to simmer 1 hour.

Add peas, mushrooms, and carrots. Simmer 15 minutes more, or until peas are heated through. Remove bouquet garni. Thicken, if necessary, with a little flour mixed with water. Add seasonings, and stir in sour cream. Heat to very hot, being careful not to boil. Stir in "C" and sprinkle with parsley. Serve with dark bread such as pumpernickel.

*A *bouquet garni* contains the aromatic herbs and spices, used to flavor soups, stews, and sauces. Tie favorite fresh or dried herbs and spices in a cheesecloth bag or tea ball. Remove the garni after cooking.

Per Serving: about 2 cups
Calories: 645
Fat: 24.3 gm
Cholesterol: 75 mg
Sodium: 565 mg
Carbohydrate: 68.6 gm
Protein: 37.6 gm

PORK CHOPS WITH APPLES
SERVES 6
170 mg vitamin C per serving

**6 lean pork chops, 1" thick
(6 oz. each, uncooked)**
**12 small whole white
onions, peeled**
**5 tart apples, quartered
and cored**
½ cup seedless raisins
1 tablespoon brown sugar
**1 cup Beef Broth
(recipe page 26)**

⅛ teaspoon thyme
⅛ teaspoon nutmeg
⅛ teaspoon mace
⅛ teaspoon ground cloves
Bouquet garni (see page 51)
1 tablespoon currant jelly
¼ teaspoon "C"

Preheat oven to 350° F.
In hot skillet, brown chops on both sides, about 5 minutes per side. Arrange
on bottom of casserole. Place onions, apple quarters, and raisins over chops.
Sprinkle with brown sugar. Add Beef Broth and season with thyme, nutmeg,
mace, and cloves. Add bouquet garni and cover casserole tightly. Bake 1
hour and 15 minutes. Remove chops to heated platter.
Discard bouquet garni and add currant jelly to sauce. Stir in "C" and pour
over chops.

Per Serving: 1 chop + ¾ cup sauce
Calories: 560
Fat: 29.5 gm
Cholesterol: 127 mg
Sodium: 154 mg
Carbohydrate: 35.9 gm
Protein: 37.3 gm

STUFFED BREAST OF VEAL

SERVES 6

189 mg vitamin C per serving • ☆ E

3 slices stale bread
6 fresh shrimp
4 cups water
6 stalks asparagus
1 cup green peas
3 tablespoons margarine
½ cup egg substitute
¼ teaspoon salt
¼ teaspoon pepper

Paprika
1 breast of veal, prepared
  for stuffing
2 cups low-sodium
  tomato or V-8 juice
½ cup nonfat sour cream
¼ teaspoon "C"
Chopped fresh parsley

Preheat oven to 350° F.

Soak bread in water until moistened (about 1-3 minutes), then squeeze and crumble to remove excess water.

Boil shrimp in water 15 minutes or until they turn bright pink and begin to float. Remove shell and devein. Set aside.

Break asparagus stalks wherever they bend most easily. Discard thick ends. Place stalks in covered saucepan with just enough water to cover bottom of pan. Cook over medium heat 10 minutes. Add peas. Steam a few minutes longer, just until the asparagus and peas are tender.

Remove from pan and set peas aside. Chop asparagus and shrimp together; then mix with wet bread crumbs. Heat margarine in saucepan; add shrimp mixture and peas. Stir gently until heated through.

Beat egg substitute. Remove pan with stuffing from heat and stir in beaten egg substitute. Season to taste with salt, pepper, and paprika.

Stuff veal breast with the mixture, and sew up or skewer opening. Place in roasting pan and pour tomato juice over veal. Roast in oven, basting frequently with tomato juice, until veal is tender and golden brown (about 1 hour and 30 minutes).

When done, remove meat to serving platter. Add sour cream to juices in pan and heat to very hot, stirring continuously. Add "C" and chopped parsley. Stir to mix, and pour into gravy boat.

Per Serving: about 4 oz. meat + ¾ cup stuffing + ½ cup sauce
Calories: 445
Fat: 24.9 gm
Cholesterol: 127 mg
Sodium: 384 mg
Carbohydrate: 17.3 gm
Protein: 37.6 gm

POT ROAST
SERVES 8
259 mg vitamin C per serving • ☆ Beta Carotene • ☆ E

Marinade:

1 cup carrots, thinly sliced
1 cup celery, thinly sliced
1 cup onions, thinly sliced
2 cloves garlic, unpeeled
  and mashed
1 tablespoon thyme
2 bay leaves
¼ cup fresh parsley, chopped

2 cloves
¼ teaspoon pepper
4 cups dry red
  wine (optional)
2 tablespoons olive oil
⅓ cup brandy (optional)

In large bowl, place plastic bag large enough to hold meat. Place all marinade ingredients into bag. Add meat to bag, twist tie, and refrigerate for 8 hours. Turn upside down in bag every hour or so.

4 pounds lean rump roast or
  bottom round of chuck, tied
4 tablespoons corn oil
1 veal knuckle, cracked

4 cups Beef Broth
  (recipe page 26)
½ teaspoon "C"
2 tablespoons flour

After marinating, remove meat, reserving marinade, and place on rack to drain. Dry thoroughly with paper towels. Unless dry, the meat will not brown.
Preheat oven to 300° F.
Heat oil in heavy Dutch oven or covered casserole just large enough to hold meat. When oil is very hot, add meat and brown on all sides, using two wooden spoons to turn meat. When browned, remove meat and pour out fat. Add marinade and reduce to half by boiling rapidly. Add veal knuckle and return meat to casserole. Add enough broth to cover two-thirds of meat.
Turn up heat until liquid just boils. Cover and place in oven. Regulate heat so that liquid barely simmers.
Cook 3 hours, or until meat can be pierced with sharp fork. When done, remove pot roast to warmed serving platter.
Pour braising juices through sieve into saucepan, forcing vegetables through with back of wooden spoon. Spoon fat off juices in pan (a bulb baster works well); then boil rapidly until about 4 cups remain.
Add rest of broth and flour mixed with a little water. Stir over medium heat until sauce thickens. Season to taste.
If sauce is not thick enough for you, add 1 tablespoon of arrowroot dis-

solved in 2 tablespoons water or port. Stir in "C."
Slice pot roast and serve sauce in heated sauce boat.

Per Serving: 6-8 oz. portion meat + vegetables
Calories: 612
Fat: 35.5 gm
Cholesterol: 183 mg
Sodium: 329 mg
Carbohydrate: 14.9 gm
Protein: 54.7 gm

EGGPLANT WITH VEAL AND MUSHROOMS

SERVES 6
10 mg vitamin C per serving • ☆ E

¼ cup corn oil
¼ cup light corn oil
   margarine, melted
1 large eggplant
¼ cup chives
1 pound ground veal
1 medium onion
1 pound mushrooms,
   finely chopped

1 whole shallot
2 cloves garlic
½ teaspoon coarse
   black pepper
½ pound low-fat cheddar
   cheese, shredded

Preheat oven to 375° F.
Hollow out eggplant and leave a ¼" border. Cut into small cubes. Heat oil
and margarine in skillet and add eggplant and veal. Cook on low heat about
3 minutes. Add onion, mushrooms, shallot, garlic, and pepper. Cook approximately 5 minutes. Add chives. Fill shell of eggplant. Top with cheese.
Bake 20 minutes. Can also be made with zucchini as an appetizer.

Per Serving: about 1½ cups
Calories: 389
Fat: 24.6 gm
Cholesterol: 86 mg
Sodium: 421 mg
Carbohydrate: 11.8 gm
Protein: 29.7 gm

QUICK CHICKEN DIVAN
SERVES 8
52 mg vitamin C per serving   •   ☆ *Beta Carotene*

**1 small bunch broccoli
(about 1 lb.)**
**12 oz. skinless sliced or
chopped chicken**
**4-5 tablespoons Parmesan
cheese**

**1 can (10 oz.) low-sodium
cream of chicken soup**
⅓ cup water

Preheat oven to 375° F.
Arrange alternate layers of cooked broccoli and leftover or canned sliced chicken in 10-x 6-x 2-inch baking dish. Sprinkle with 2 tablespoons grated Parmesan cheese. Top with another layer of cooked broccoli. Mix cream of chicken soup with water. Heat and pour over broccoli and sprinkle with 2-3 tablespoons grated Parmesan cheese. Bake 20-30 minutes.

Per Serving: about 1 cup
Calories: 131
Fat: 5.3 gm
Cholesterol 42 mg
Sodium: 174 mg
Carbohydrate: 4.9 gm
Protein: 16 gm

CHICKEN AND GREEN PEPPERS
SERVES 6
200 mg vitamin C per serving

¼ cup olive oil
¼ cup corn oil margarine
**2 (2½ lbs.) chickens cut up,
skinless**
1 lemon
¼ teaspoon salt
¼ teaspoon pepper

**2 green peppers, seeded and
cut into strips**
8 shallots, finely chopped
**½ cup dry white
wine (optional)**
¼ teaspoon "C"

Melt oil and margarine in deep skillet. Rub chicken with cut lemon, salt, and pepper. Brown chicken, a few pieces at a time, turning it with tongs. Begin with dark meat, since it takes longer to cook. Add green peppers and shallots. Cook 3 minutes. Cover pan and cook 15-20 minutes.

Remove chicken to heated platter. Add wine to vegetables and bring to boil. Boil 1 minute, turn off heat. Stir in "C." Adjust seasoning if necessary, and pour over chicken.

Per Serving: ⅓ chicken
Calories: 642
Fat: 43.9 gm
Cholesterol: 176 mg
Sodium: 330 mg
Carbohydrate: 5.2 gm
Protein: 55.3 gm

CHICKEN MARENGO

SERVES 4
135 mg vitamin C per serving

4 tablespoons olive oil
1 (2 lbs.) chicken, cut in serving pieces, skinned
1 lemon
¼ teaspoon salt
¼ teaspoon pepper
2 tablespoons flour
½ cup Chicken Broth (recipe page 28)

½ cup Madeira wine (optional)
1 clove garlic, finely chopped
1 tablespoon tomato paste
Bouquet garni (see page 51)
½ pound mushrooms, thickly sliced
⅛ teaspoon "C"

Heat oil in deep skillet. Rub chicken with cut lemon, salt, and pepper. Brown chicken in oil over medium heat. Add a few pieces at a time, starting with dark meat. When all sides are crispy, remove chicken to heated platter. Remove skillet from heat and stir in flour. Return to heat and cook flour for 2 minutes, stirring constantly and being careful not to burn.
Using wire whisk, stir in broth, wine, garlic, tomato paste, and bouquet garni. Cook 3 minutes, stirring frequently. Add mushrooms and return chicken to skillet. Cover and simmer gently for 1 hour. Remove bouquet garni; stir in "C." Adjust seasonings if necessary.

Per Serving: ¼ chicken
Calories: 520
Fat: 34.7 gm
Cholesterol: 99 mg
Sodium: 334 mg
Carbohydrate: 7.9 gm
Protein: 42.4 gm

SAUTÉED CHICKEN WITH PARSLEY

SERVES 6
177 mg vitamin C per serving • ☆ E

2 (2½ lbs.) chickens cut
  up, skinless
1 lemon, cut in half
¼ teaspoon salt
¼ teaspoon pepper

¼ cup corn oil margarine
½ cup dry white
  wine (optional)
¼ cup chopped fresh parsley
¼ teaspoon "C"

Rub chicken pieces with cut lemon, salt, and pepper. Heat margarine in a large pan until bubbling, but do not allow to brown. Brown chicken pieces quickly on all sides.

Cover pan, reduce heat, and continue to cook until chicken is done (30-45 minutes). Since white meat cooks faster than dark, remove it to heated platter first.

After all chicken has been removed to heated platter, add wine to pan and boil quickly, scraping with wooden spoon any pieces that have stuck to pan.

Stir in chopped parsley and "C." Pour over chicken.

Per Serving: ⅓ chicken + sauce
Calories: 539
Fat: 34.5 gm
Cholesterol: 132 mg
Sodium: 325 mg
Carbohydrate: 1.5 gm
Protein: 54.5 gm

CURRIED ALMOND CHICKEN

MAKES ABOUT 24 (1") BALLS
trace vitamin C per serving • ☆ E

½ cup chopped almonds,
  toasted
1 can (6½ oz.)
  boned chicken
1 package (3 oz.) nonfat
  cream cheese, softened

2 tablespoons chutney
1 teaspoon curry powder
¼ teaspoon pepper
¼ cup minced parsley

Finely chop almonds; set aside. In small bowl, combine chicken and cream cheese, breaking up any large chunks of chicken. Add chutney, curry powder, and almonds; mix until well blended; pepper to taste. Chill until mixture is firm, about one hour. Shape into 1-inch balls and roll in minced parsley. Chill until ready to serve.

Per Serving: 4 balls
Calories: 183
Fat: 11.6 gm
Cholesterol: 18 mg
Sodium: 194 mg
Carbohydrate: 7.2 gm
Protein: 12.3 gm

MELVA'S GOURMET BAKED SALMON

SERVES 6
29 mg vitamin C per serving • ☆ *Beta Carotene* • ☆ *E*

2 large onions, sliced
1 clove garlic, minced
3 stalks celery, chopped, including tops
½ cup corn oil
3 green onions, chopped
2 tablespoons chopped parsley

½ cup dry white wine
1 can (1 lb.) whole tomatoes, crushed
¼ teaspoon salt
¼ teaspoon pepper
3 pounds salmon steaks

Preheat oven to 375° F.
Sauté onions, garlic, and celery in oil 10 minutes. Add remaining ingredients except salmon. Place salmon in large casserole. Pour mixture over salmon. Bake, covered, 20-30 minutes.

Per Serving: 6 oz. salmon + sauce
Calories: 633
Fat: 43.0 gm
Cholesterol: 134 mg
Sodium: 420 mg
Carbohydrate: 12.7 gm
Protein: 47.2 gm

CARROT-TOPPED COD FISH

SERVES 6
6 mg vitamin C per serving • ☆ Beta Carotene • ☆ E

2 cups coarsely shredded carrots
3 tablespoons corn oil margarine
1 teaspoon grated lemon peel
2 tablespoons lemon juice

¼ teaspoon thyme
¼ teaspoon salt
2 pounds cod, cut into
** 6 equal portions**

Preheat oven to 450° F.
Combine first 6 ingredients. Place cod in pan and cover with carrot mixture.
Cover tightly with foil and bake 8-10 minutes or until fish flakes.
Garnish with celery leaves, if desired.

Per Serving: 4.3 oz. cod + sauce
Calories: 187
Fat: 6.6 gm
Cholesterol: 66 mg
Sodium: 237 mg
Carbohydrate: 4.3 gm
Protein: 27.4 gm

BAKED FISH & VEGETABLE DINNER

SERVES 6
90 mg vitamin C per serving • ☆ Beta Carotene • ☆ E

3 large potatoes, peeled
** and sliced thin**
½ pound fresh mushrooms,
** sliced**
1 cup carrots, sliced
1 cup green pepper, diced
1 cup red pepper, diced
4 large tomatoes, peeled,
** seeded, and sliced**
2 green onions, sliced thin
1½ pounds fish fillets
** (haddock, perch, scrod,**
** flounder, or sole)**

2 tablespoons corn oil
** margarine, melted**
1 teaspoon fresh thyme,
** chopped, or ½**
** teaspoon, dried**
1 teaspoon fresh basil,
** chopped or ½ teaspoon,**
** dried**
¼ teaspoon pepper,
** freshly ground**
Lemon slices

Preheat oven to 350° F. Generously oil 2-quart baking dish. Arrange potatoes in dish and sprinkle lightly with salt substitute. Cover with foil and bake 15 minutes. Uncover and place mushrooms, carrots, green pepper, red pepper, tomatoes, and onions over partially cooked potatoes. Place fish fillets over vegetables, and make a few diagonal cuts in fish. Dribble melted margarine over fish and sprinkle with herbs, salt (optional), and pepper. Bake, uncovered, until fish is lightly browned and flakes easily. This may take 10-20 minutes, depending on thickness of fillets. Do not overcook. Garnish with lemon slices.

Per Serving: 2 cups
Calories: 361
Fat: 2.7 gm
Cholesterol: 54 mg (will vary depending on fish)
Sodium: 176 mg
Carbohydrate: 48.9 gm
Protein: 27.6 gm

TUNA 'N RICE GRILLED PEPPERS

SERVES 2
152 mg vitamin C per serving • ☆ E

1 can (6½ oz.) tuna in natural spring water, drained
2 cups cooked long-grain rice, warm (no salt added in cooking)
1 red and 1 green bell pepper
4 onion slices
¼ cup fresh basil leaves, chopped

2 tablespoons corn oil
1½ tablespoons fresh lemon juice
1 tablespoon fresh parsley, minced
Freshly ground pepper
Radishes, olives, basil sprigs to garnish

Grill, seed, and dice peppers. Grill and dice onion slices. Grilling may be done on a barbecue or under broiler flame.
In large bowl, combine all ingredients except garnishes. Cover and cool to room temperature. Garnish with radishes, olives, and basil.

Per Serving: 2¼ cups each
Calories: 593
Fat: 29.5 gm
Cholesterol: 38 mg
Sodium: 381 mg
Carbohydrate: 57.5 gm
Protein: 24.2 gm

POACHED CODFISH IN MUSTARD SAUCE

SERVES 6
170 mg vitamin C per serving   •   ☆ E

2½ **pounds (6) fresh
  codfish steaks**
2½ **cups water**
1 **medium onion, quartered**
1 **bay leaf, crushed**
¼ **teaspoon pepper**
3 **tablespoons corn
  oil margarine**

3 **tablespoons all-purpose
  flour**
¼ **cup Dijon mustard**
1 **tablespoon lemon juice**
¼ **teaspoon "C"**
Sprigs fresh parsley

Wipe codfish steaks with damp cloth. Arrange in single layer in large skillet with tight-fitting cover.

Add water, onion, bay leaf, and pepper. Bring to boil. Reduce heat, cover, and simmer 8 minutes, until fish flakes easily with fork. Remove fish and reserve liquid. Remove bay leaf. Place steaks on heated serving platter and keep warm.

Melt margarine in saucepan. When it begins to bubble, remove from heat and stir in flour until smooth. Return to heat and add 2 cups of strained fish liquid. Bring sauce to boil, stirring constantly. Reduce heat and add mustard, lemon juice, "C," and salt, if desired.

Garnish fish steaks with parsley and serve sauce separately.

Per Serving: 5-6 oz. fish with sauce
Calories: 235
Fat: 7.6 gm
Cholesterol: 82 mg
Sodium: 454 mg
Carbohydrate: 5.6 gm
Protein: 34.4 gm

SEVICHE

SERVES 6
135 mg vitamin C per serving

¾ cup strained fresh
   lemon juice
¾ cup strained fresh
   lime juice
1 tablespoon chili powder
½ teaspoon minced garlic
½ teaspoon hot pepper sauce
¼ teaspoon salt
¼ teaspoon freshly
   ground pepper
¼ teaspoon "C"
1½ pounds fillets of sole,
   flounder, or other firm,
   white fish (fillets should
   be cut into 2" pieces)

½ green pepper, seeded
   and cut into 2" pieces
½ sweet red pepper, seeded
   and cut into 2" pieces
1 medium red onion,
   thinly sliced into rings
2 leaves Boston lettuce
2 tablespoons chopped
   fresh parsley

About selection of fish for this recipe: Only fresh fish can be used, not frozen. If you are buying fillets, be sure to select those that are at least ¼-inch thick; otherwise, they may break up and disintegrate while marinating.

Combine lemon and lime juices, chili powder, garlic, hot pepper sauce, salt, pepper, and "C" in a glass or ceramic dish—one large enough to hold all fish in one layer. Mix thoroughly with wire whisk. Lay fish side by side in marinade.

Place pieces of peppers and onion rings over fish. Marinade should completely cover fish, peppers, and onions. If it does not, add more lemon and lime juice, in equal amounts.

Cover dish tightly with plastic wrap, refrigerate at least 4 hours, until fish becomes white and opaque and is "cooked." The longer fish is marinated, the richer the flavor. Seviche can be safely kept in refrigerator up to 3 days.

When ready to serve, place one or two lettuce leaves on chilled plate. Fill with Seviche and garnish with chopped parsley and tomato wedges, if desired.

Per Serving: 4 oz. fish with ⅓ cup peppers/onions topping
Calories: 151
Fat: 1.8 gm
Cholesterol: 54 mg
Sodium: 209 mg
Carbohydrate: 10.4 gm
Protein: 22.8 gm

FILLETS OF SOLE WITH TARRAGON-CHIVE BUTTER

SERVES 6
170 mg vitamin C per serving

2 pounds fresh fillets of sole
¼ cup corn oil margarine,
  softened, divided
2 tablespoons lemon juice
1 tablespoon, coarsely
  chopped fresh tarragon or
  1 teaspoon chopped
  dried tarragon

1 tablespoon fresh or frozen
  chopped chives
¼ teaspoon "C"

Preheat oven to 350° F.

Coat fillets with margarine. Sprinkle with lemon juice. Arrange side by side in greased baking dish. Cover dish with foil and bake 15-20 minutes, until fish flakes easily with fork. Remove to heated serving platter.

Combine remaining margarine with tarragon and chives. Heat, add "C," and pour over fillets.

Per Serving: 4-5 oz. sole + sauce
Calories: 201
Fat: 9.2 gm
Cholesterol: 72 mg
Sodium: 190 mg
Carbohydrate: 0.6 gm
Protein: 28.6 gm

SALMON MOUSSE

SERVES 6
170 mg vitamin C per serving

2 teaspoons corn oil
1 envelope unflavored
gelatin
¼ cup dry white
wine (optional)
¾ cup Chicken Broth
(recipe page 28)
2 cups canned salmon, drained,
firmly packed, chilled

2 teaspoons tomato paste
1 teaspoon paprika
1 tablespoon onion,
finely minced
1 tablespoon lemon juice
¼ teaspoon "C"
5 drops hot pepper sauce
½ cup evaporated skim
milk

Lightly oil 2- or 3-cup mold. Wipe out excess oil with paper towel.

Soften gelatin in wine 5 minutes. Meanwhile, simmer Chicken Broth. When gelatin is softened, add to broth and cook 1-2 minutes until gelatin totally dissolves. Pour into blender. Add salmon and purée on high speed until smooth. Scrape into small mixing bowl and stir in tomato paste, paprika, onion, lemon juice, "C," and hot pepper sauce. Correct seasoning if necessary.

Whip skim milk in chilled bowl until it is firm, but not quite stiff. Set bowl of salmon purée in large bowl with ice and a little cold water. Stir until mixture begins to stiffen—this doesn't take long. Gently fold in whipped milk. Do not overmix; just fold until white streaks disappear. Pour into oiled mold. Smooth off top and cover with plastic wrap.

Refrigerate 3 hours or overnight.

Just before serving, unmold mousse onto a serving platter by running a sharp knife around edge of mold. Turn it over onto platter. Cover mold with wet hot towel for a moment. Tap mold on bottom to dislodge.

If this doesn't work, place hot towel over mold and try again.

Serve with homemade Mayonnaise (recipe page 143).

Per Serving: ¾-1 cup
Calories: 146
Fat: 6.0 gm
Cholesterol: 28 mg
Sodium: 371 mg
Carbohydrate: 4.1 gm
Protein: 16.9 gm

POACHED HALIBUT STEAKS WITH TARTARE SAUCE

SERVES 6
267 mg vitamin C per serving • ☆ E

6 (½ lb.) halibut steaks
1 onion, thinly sliced
6 sprigs fresh parsley
1 large bay leaf
2 whole cloves
¼ teaspoon thyme

3 tablespoons white
   wine vinegar
½ teaspoon tarragon
1 recipe Tartare Sauce
   (recipe below)

In medium saucepan, bring 4-5 cups water to boil. Place steaks in large skillet. Add onion, parsley, bay leaf, cloves, thyme, vinegar, and tarragon. Add boiling water to cover. Bring to boil and simmer gently for about 10 minutes. Remove bay leaf. Remove steaks carefully and arrange on heated serving platter. Serve with Tartare Sauce.

Per Serving: ½ lb. steak + ¼ cup sauce
Calories: 527
Fat: 35.3 gm
Cholesterol: 103 mg
Sodium: 180 mg
Carbohydrate: 3.3 gm
Protein: 48.6 gm

TARTARE SAUCE

SERVES 6 (1½ CUPS)
165 mg vitamin C per serving • ☆ E

1 teaspoon fresh parsley,
   finely chopped
1 teaspoon shallots,
   finely chopped
¼ teaspoon dried tarragon
   leaves, chopped
1 teaspoon gherkins,
   finely chopped

1 teaspoon green olives,
   finely chopped
¼ teaspoon pepper,
   freshly ground
1 teaspoon Dijon mustard
1 cup Mayonnaise
   (recipe page 143)

Combine all ingredients in mixing bowl. Chill until ready to serve.

Per Serving: ¼ cup
Calories: 278
Fat: 30.1 gm
Cholesterol: 29 mg
Sodium: 56 mg
Carbohydrate: 0.7 gm
Protein: 1.0 gm

COLD POACHED SALMON STEAKS WITH GREEN MAYONNAISE

SERVES 6
170 mg vitamin C per serving   •   ☆ E

**2 tablespoons corn
  oil margarine**
1 medium onion, chopped
2 medium carrots, chopped
2 stalks celery, chopped
4 cups water
**½ cup dry white wine
  (optional)**

8 peppercorns
**6 small salmon steaks,
  1" thick**
**1 recipe Green Mayonnaise
  (recipe page 143)**

Heat margarine in large skillet and add onion, carrots, and celery. Sauté
5 minutes. Add water, wine, and peppercorns. Simmer 5 minutes.
Place salmon steaks gently into liquid. Keeping heat on low, cover, and gently simmer 8-12 minutes, or until flesh barely flakes with fork. Remove
salmon carefully. Cool, then refrigerate. Serve chilled with Green Mayonnaise.

Per Serving: 3-4 oz. steak + ¼ cup vegetable + 5 tablespoons Green Mayonnaise Sauce
Calories: 610
Fat: 54.2 gm
Cholesterol: 103 mg
Sodium: 93 mg
Carbohydrate: 4.7 gm
Protein: 24.5 gm

BROILED SWORDFISH WITH COLD CUCUMBER SAUCE

SERVES 6
178 mg vitamin C per serving   •   ☆ E

2½ **pounds fresh swordfish,
cut 1" thick, room
temperature**
3 **tablespoons lemon juice**
2 **tablespoons corn
oil margarine**

¼ **teaspoon salt**
¼ **teaspoon pepper**
Freshly ground pepper
1 **recipe Cold Cucumber
Sauce (recipe below)**

Preheat broiler.
Rub steaks with lemon juice.
Place swordfish on margarine-coated broiler rack. Spread 1 tablespoon of margarine over fish and sprinkle with salt and pepper. Rack should be 3 inches below heat. Broil 3 minutes and brush again with margarine.
Turn fish over very carefully so it does not break. Brush with margarine, salt, and pepper. Continue broiling for another 4-5 minutes, brushing once or twice with margarine until fish is quite brown and firm to touch. Transfer to hot platter. Serve at once with Cold Cucumber Sauce.

Per Serving: about 6 oz. swordfish + ½ cup sauce
Calories: 343
Fat: 11.8 gm
Cholesterol: 76 mg
Sodium: 406 mg
Carbohydrate: 15.6 gm
Protein: 43.3 gm

COLD CUCUMBER SAUCE

SERVES 6 (3¼ CUPS)
178 mg vitamin C per serving

1 **pint nonfat sour cream**
2 **teaspoons white wine
vinegar**
Dash cayenne
¼ **teaspoon "C"**

2 **teaspoons grated onion**
3 **tablespoons fresh dill,
finely chopped**
1 **cup cucumber, peeled,
seeded, diced**

Combine sour cream, vinegar, cayenne, "C," and grated onion in mixing bowl. When thoroughly mixed, add chopped dill and diced cucumber. Taste for seasoning. Chill until ready to serve.

Per Serving: ½ cup
Calories: 88
Fat: 0.5 gm
Cholesterol: trace
Sodium: 110 mg
Carbohydrate: 14.9 gm
Protein: 5.8 gm

HALIBUT CREOLE POTATO TOPPER

SERVES 4
53 mg vitamin C per serving • ☆ E

- **1 cup carrots, diced**
- **¼ cup onion, chopped**
- **4 teaspoons corn oil**
- **1 tablespoon corn oil margarine**
- **1 can (16 oz.) diced tomatoes**
- **¼ cup chopped green pepper**
- **½ teaspoon thyme, crushed**
- **½ teaspoon chili powder**
- **¼ teaspoon salt, if desired**
- **1 pound Alaska halibut, thawed, boned, skinned, and cubed**
- **¼ teaspoon pepper**
- **4 (8 oz.) potatoes, baked**

Sauté carrots and onion in oil and margarine until just tender. Stir in tomatoes, green pepper, thyme, chili powder, and salt. Bring to boil; add halibut and cook until halibut flakes when tested with fork. Season with pepper. Slit baked potatoes lengthwise and open by gently squeezing from bottom. Spoon ¼ halibut mixture over each potato.

Per Serving: 1 potato + 1½ cup topping
Calories: 503
Fat: 10.3 gm
Cholesterol: 37 mg
Sodium: 457 mg
Carbohydrate: 69.9 gm
Protein: 32.4 gm

THAI-STYLE SALMON POTATO TOPPER

SERVES 4

101 mg vitamin C per serving • ☆ *Beta Carotene* • ☆ *E*

½ cup onion, vertically sliced
1 tablespoon fresh ginger
  root, slivered
¼-½ teaspoon red pepper,
  crushed
1 tablespoon corn oil
1 pound Alaska salmon,
  thawed if necessary, skinned,
  boned, and cubed
2 cups broccoli florets
1 cup pea pods
1 cup tofu cubes
1 cup cucumber, vertically
  sliced, seeded if desired

2 shiitake mushrooms,
  rehydrated and thinly
  sliced (about ¼ cup)
¾ cup water
¼ cup vinegar
4 teaspoons packed
  brown sugar
1 tablespoon cornstarch
1 teaspoon grated lemon peel
¼ teaspoon salt
¼ teaspoon pepper
4 Washington Russet
  potatoes (8 oz. each),
  baked

Sauté onion, ginger root, and red pepper in oil until onion is tender; add salmon and cook 3 minutes. Add broccoli, pea pods, tofu, cucumber, and mushrooms; cook until vegetables are just tender. Combine water, vinegar, brown sugar, cornstarch, lemon peel, salt, and pepper; stir into vegetables. Cook until mixture thickens and boils. Slit baked potatoes lengthwise and open by gently squeezing from bottom. Spoon ¼ salmon mixture over each potato.

Per Serving: 1 potato + 1¾-2 cups topping
Calories: 630
Fat: 19.0 gm
Cholesterol: 75 mg
Sodium: 223 mg
Carbohydrate: 75.2 gm
Protein: 38.0 gm

STIR-FRIED TURKEY AND ASPARAGUS

SERVES 4
34 mg vitamin C per serving • ☆ E

1½ tablespoons dry sherry
2½ tablespoons low-sodium
  soy sauce
½ teaspoon ground ginger
3 garlic cloves, minced
1½ bunches green onions,
  white and green parts,
  thinly sliced (about ¾ cup)
1 pound turkey breast, raw,
  boneless, thinly sliced

2 tablespoons canola or
  sunflower oil
¼-½ pound fresh
  asparagus or green beans,
  cut into 1" slices
¼ pound fresh mushrooms,
  sliced
¼ pound fresh bean sprouts
1 tablespoon lemon juice
¼ teaspoon pepper, if desired

In small bowl, combine sherry, soy sauce, ginger, garlic, green onions, and turkey. Refrigerate at least 30 minutes. Heat oil in wok or large skillet over medium-high heat; add onions and garlic. Stir-fry about 30 seconds. Add asparagus; stir to coat. Stir in turkey and continue cooking until meat turns from pink to light brown. Stir in mushrooms and bean sprouts; cook 1 minute longer. Stir in 1 tablespoon soy sauce and ¼ teaspoon ginger, plus lemon juice and pepper if desired.
Serve immediately.

Per Serving: about 2 cups
Calories: 262
Fat: 10.2 gm
Cholesterol: 59 mg
Sodium: 259 mg
Carbohydrate: 10.3 gm
Protein: 30.2 gm

BARBECUE SAUCE

SERVES 6 (1¾ CUPS)
160 mg vitamin C per serving

¼ **cup vinegar**
½ **cup water**
2 **tablespoons honey**
½ **teaspoon salt (optional)**
1 **tablespoon prepared**
  mustard
½ **teaspoon pepper**
¼ **teaspoon cayenne**

1 **thick lemon slice**
1 **medium onion, thinly**
  sliced
¼ **cup corn oil margarine**
2 **tablespoons Worcestershire**
  sauce
½ **cup catsup**
¼ **teaspoon "C"**

Mix vinegar, water, honey, salt, mustard, pepper, cayenne, lemon slice, onion slices, and margarine in saucepan. Simmer 20 minutes. Add Worcestershire, catsup, and bring to boil. Just before serving, stir in "C." Serve this sauce hot with spareribs, short ribs, chicken, or use as a baster during the last 10 minutes of cooking.

Per Serving: about ¼ cup
Calories: 137
Fat: 7.6 gm
Cholesterol: 0 mg
Sodium: 603 mg
Carbohydrate: 16.2 gm
Protein: 0.5 gm

WATERCRESS SAUCE

SERVES 4 (1 CUP)
174 mg vitamin C per serving • ☆ *E*

1 **cup watercress**
¾ **cup Mayonnaise (recipe page 143)**

2 **tablespoons chili sauce**

Blend watercress and Mayonnaise on medium speed until mixed. Strain sauce through fine sieve. Stir in chili sauce. Serve with cold cooked fish or shellfish.

Per Serving: about ¼ cup
Calories: 317
Fat: 33.5 gm
Cholesterol: 32 mg
Sodium: 121 mg
Carbohydrate: 2.1 gm
Protein: 1.3 gm

CLAM AND TOMATO SAUCE

SERVES 6 (3 CUPS)
195 mg vitamin C per serving • ☆ Beta Carotene

½ cup olive oil
2 cloves garlic, minced
1 can (6 oz.) low-sodium
   tomato paste
2½ cups stewed tomatoes
¼ teaspoon pepper
⅛ teaspoon thyme

⅛ teaspoon oregano
1 can (7 oz.) minced
   clams, drained
¼ cup fresh parsley,
   finely chopped
¼ teaspoon "C"

Heat oil in large skillet. Add garlic and cook over medium heat until garlic turns golden. Stir in tomato paste, stewed tomatoes, pepper, thyme, and oregano. Cook 2 minutes.

Add clams and parsley. Cook 2-3 minutes more and add "C."

Serve with 1 pound spaghetti noodles cooked *al dente*, which literally means "to the tooth," offering a slight resistance when bitten into.

Per Serving: ½ cup
Calories: 258
Fat: 19.5 gm
Cholesterol: 8 mg
Sodium: 710 mg
Carbohydrate: 14.1 gm
Protein: 6.3 gm

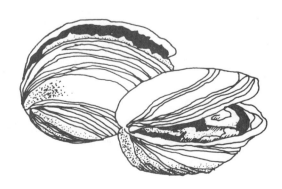

Vegetables

This is one of the most important sections of our *Antioxidant Cookbook*, simply because the vitamins C and beta carotene, and to some extent E, are so bountifully supplied in vegetables by nature, but we in our "civilized" way stew and simmer original antioxidant potency right out of food.

Once again, careful shopping habits are very important as a start. In no other area of food procurement is there such a huge variation in quality, and, of course, in vitamin content that goes with it.

The combination of mediocre-quality supermarket vegetables and overcooking is one of America's greatest nutritional disasters. This is particularly so because vegetables contain more vitamin C and beta carotene than any other single category of food. How many people pay sky-high prices for pithy, soft vegetables, take them home, soak them, peel them, cook them in boiling salted water until they nearly fall apart, and then confidently serve them?

First of all, even the best of vegetables obtainable at most markets leave a lot to be desired. They've been sprayed, waxed, and shipped for days from one state to another.

Second, vitamin C, like sugar in vegetables, is highly soluble in water, so much of the vitamin disappears into soaking water, especially if the vegetable has been cut or sliced.

Third, discarded peeling carries away with it flavors and nutrients that are heavily concentrated next to the skin.

Fourth, long boiling times extract more vitamin C and other nutrients into water. The loss is accelerated even more by salt in water. And then the water, which by now may contain more vitamins than the vegetables themselves, is thrown out. What is left is a sodden, tasteless pulp containing practically no vitamin A, C, or E, or any other nutrient, for that matter!

If you are able to have your own garden, or know a grocer who carries really fresh vegetables, you are indeed fortunate. Even if you must settle for second best, your vegetables will retain more vitamin C and taste better if you follow some simple rules in preparation. The very best way to preserve flavor and vitamin C in vegetables is to wash them in cold water, scrub lightly, dry, and store in the refrigerator until ready to eat. Then slice, season, and serve—raw.

The next best way to preserve flavor and vitamin C is to follow the above preparation method, but cook as little as possible, seasoning just before serving. This is the method we've used in this section. Do not add baking soda to preserve color in green vegetables as baking soda will reduce the vitamin C level and also modify flavor and texture. The utensil you use for cooking vegetables should be one with a tight-fitting lid to retain steam and prevent oxygen from reaching the vegetable, so constructed that it heats from both the bottom and the sides. A pan with a heavy aluminum bottom and sides and a stainless steel lining is probably best, although there are others—ceramic coated, for example. But note that copper or iron utensils may cause loss of vitamin E.

Now for the question of whether or not to peel the vegetable. We are not faddists. Taste and texture are extremely important to good food. If the vegetable skin is tough or bitter (tomatoes and some root vegetables, for example), you should be willing to forgo the nutrients lost by peeling. But not completely. If you will refer to the recipe on Vegetable Broth (page 27), you will see we recommend you toss leftover vegetables, clean peelings, and green tops into a plastic bag kept in the freezer, to be used later for vegetable broth.

A note on frozen vegetables: They may be used in place of fresh ones in the following recipes. Before cooking, break apart vegetables. Then place in a pan with ½ cup of water. Cover tightly. Steam over moderate heat until tender (8-10 minutes). Add "C" after vegetables are cooked. (See Appendix for a more extensive list of sources of vitamins C, beta carotene, and E.)

STEAMED ASPARAGUS
SERVES 1
24 mg vitamin C per serving

Remove ends of asparagus stalks by bending stalk near bottom; wherever it begins to break, snap it off. The break occurs just above tough part of stalk.
Be sure to clean asparagus thoroughly as they are often very sandy. Rinse quickly under cold running water.
Steam asparagus by laying them across steamer (flat). They should be done in 8 minutes or slightly more if they are very thick. Test for doneness by pricking with fork.
They can be served hot with hollandaise or cold with Mayonnaise (recipe page 143) or Vinaigrette Dressing (recipe page 121), any of which will add more vitamin C.

Per Serving: 6 asparagus, plain
Calories: 25
Fat: 0.2 gm
Cholesterol: 0 mg
Sodium: 2 mg
Carbohydrate: 3.9 gm
Protein: 1.9 gm

ALMOND ASPARAGUS
SERVES 4
38 mg vitamin C per serving • ☆ E

1 pound asparagus
2 tablespoons corn
  oil margarine
1 tablespoon lemon juice

½ cup blanched slivered
  almonds, toasted
¼ teaspoon pepper

Wash asparagus; cut into 1-inch diagonal slices. Heat margarine in skillet; add asparagus and sauté three to four minutes. Cover skillet and steam about two minutes. Toss asparagus with lemon juice and almonds; pepper to taste.

Per Serving: about 1 cup
Calories: 195
Fat: 14.6 gm
Cholesterol: 0 mg
Sodium: 53 mg
Carbohydrate: 9.5 gm
Protein: 6.3 gm

STEAMED ARTICHOKES
SERVES 1
8 mg vitamin C per serving

Be sure to select only those artichokes that are tightly closed—they are freshest, tastier, and, of course, have maximum natural vitamin C.

Trim stem very close to base so that artichoke has a flat bottom to rest on. To remove hairy choke (it is inedible) before cooking, cut 1 inch off top with sharp knife. Spread leaves open with your fingers—as wide as possible—and pull out small yellow-green leaves (they usually come out all at once). Then with spoon, scrape all hairy choke away. If you'd rather, you can remove choke after cooking or let everyone do his own. Cooking time will be slightly longer (about 5 minutes) if choke is not removed beforehand.

Remove sharp points of leaves with scissors.

Steam artichoke for approximately 15 minutes, or until tender. Test heart with fork or pull off one of leaves; if it comes off easily, artichoke is done. Use deep saucepan, with steaming rack in bottom—one that is deep enough so artichokes will fit tightly and can be tightly covered.

Artichokes can be served hot, warm, or cold with a variety of sauces. We recommend one of our favorite sauces: Mayonnaise (recipe page 143) and Vinaigrette Dressing (recipe page 121) not only because each complements artichoke so well, but because the sauces provide additional vitamin C. Sauces can be served in separate dishes or in hollowed-out center of artichoke.

Per Serving: 1 artichoke, plain
Calories: 73
Fat: 0.2 gm
Cholesterol: 0 mg
Sodium: 114 mg
Carbohydrate: 13.4 gm
Protein: 4.2 gm

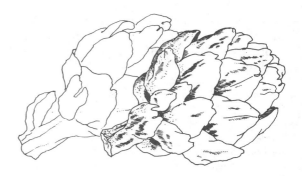

HERBED TOMATO CORKSCREW PASTA

SERVES 4
76 mg vitamin C per serving • ☆ E

2 red peppers
1 (16 oz.) can no-salt-added
 whole tomatoes
⅓ cup fresh parsley sprigs
2 tablespoons red-wine
 vinegar
1 tablespoon olive oil
2 teaspoons salt-free extra
 spicy seasoning mixture

2 cups zucchini or yellow
 squash, thinly sliced
½ pound fusilli, cooked
 al dente and drained
1 ounce (¼ cup) sliced
 almonds, preferably
 toasted

Preheat broiler. Cut each pepper lengthwise into 4 pieces. Discard stems and seeds. Set pieces on aluminum foil and place about 4 inches from boiler element. Broil until skin is well charred. Put into plastic bag using tongs; seal and let peppers steam 5 minutes. Rinse under cool water; peel off and discard skins.

Combine peppers, tomatoes, parsley, vinegar, oil, and spice mixture in blender or food processor. Process to make coarse purée. Set aside.

Heat 1 inch water in medium saucepan fitted with vegetable steamer. Steam zucchini until just tender. Drain and set aside.

In bowl, combine zucchini, pasta, and half of tomato sauce. Spoon onto individual dishes and sprinkle with sliced almonds. Serve warm.

Per Serving: about 2 cups
Calories: 343
Fat: 9.2 gm
Cholesterol: 0 mg
Sodium: 64 mg
Carbohydrate: 53.6 gm
Protein: 7.5 gm

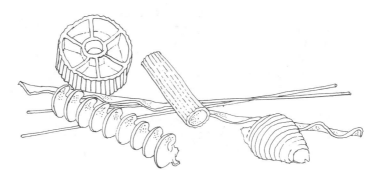

GREEN BEANS WITH ALMONDS

SERVES 6

170 mg vitamin C per serving • ☆ E

2 pounds fresh green beans	**¼ teaspoon salt**
1 cup whole or sliced	**¼ teaspoon "C"**
blanched almonds	
2 tablespoons corn	
oil margarine	

Rinse beans under cold water. Snap off ends. Pat dry.

Steam for 10-12 minutes until tender, but slightly crunchy. Drain thoroughly.

While beans are steaming, sauté almonds lightly in margarine. Shake pan often to move almonds around. Brown nuts slightly and salt to taste.

They should have toasted flavor.

Return beans to saucepan in which they were cooked and heat. Add almonds, margarine, and "C." Stir and serve immediately.

Per Serving: about 1-1¼ cups
Calories: 233
Fat: 15.7 gm
Cholesterol: 0 mg
Sodium: 138 mg
Carbohydrate: 15.3 gm
Protein: 7.4 gm

GREEN BEANS WITH PEPPERS AND ONIONS

SERVES 6

185 mg vitamin C per serving

1½ pounds fresh green beans	**¼ cup boiling water**
2 tablespoons corn oil	**¼ teaspoon salt**
1 clove garlic, crushed	**1 teaspoon dried basil**
1 tablespoon onion, chopped	**¼ teaspoon "C"**
¾ cup sweet red pepper,	**½ cup grated low-fat**
diced	**Parmesan cheese**

Snap ends off beans, rinse under cold water, and cut into 1-inch pieces. Heat oil and garlic in heavy skillet. Add onion and red pepper and cook slowly 3-4 minutes. Add beans, water, salt, basil. Cover and simmer until beans are tender, 8-10 minutes. Sprinkle in "C" and stir in half cheese. Sprinkle remaining cheese over beans when served.

Per Serving: about 1 cup
Calories: 127
Fat: 7.2 gm
Cholesterol: 6 mg
Sodium: 250 mg
Carbohydrate: 9.7 gm
Protein: 5.7 gm

GREEN BEANS PROVENÇALE
SERVES 8
200 mg vitamin C per serving

2 cups onions, thinly sliced
2 tablespoons olive oil
6 large, firm, ripe tomatoes,
  peeled, seeded, juiced,
  and chopped
¾ cup liquid from tomatoes,
  plus water

2 pounds fresh green beans
¼ teaspoon "C"
¼ teaspoon salt
¼ teaspoon pepper
¼ cup fresh parsley,
  chopped
*Bouquet Garni (see page 51)

Using large skillet, cook onions in olive oil until tender and transparent. This will take about 10 minutes. Add tomatoes, bouquet garni, and liquid, and continue simmering for 30 minutes. Remove bouquet garni.
While tomatoes are cooking, snap ends off beans and rinse under cold water. Steam beans for approximately 5 minutes. Toss them in pan with tomatoes and onions and simmer, covered, for 8 minutes until beans are just tender. Most of juice will have evaporated by this time. If juice has not evaporated, remove beans with slotted spoon, turn heat up to high, and boil liquid off rapidly. Return beans to pan.
Sprinkle "C" over beans and season to taste with salt and pepper. Toss beans with chopped parsley and serve.

Per Serving: about 1½-1¾ cups
Calories: 115
Fat: 4.1 gm
Cholesterol: 0 mg
Sodium: 85 mg
Carbohydrate: 15.9 gm
Protein: 3.4 gm

HARVARD BEETS

SERVES 6
170 mg vitamin C per serving

12 small fresh beets
½ cup granulated sugar
2 teaspoons cornstarch
½ cup vinegar

¼ teaspoon "C"
2 tablespoons margarine,
  softened

Gently wash beets. Cut off tops, leaving about an inch attached to beet. Do not peel. (If you pierce skin before cooking, beet juice and color will disappear into cooking water.) Steam beets for 30-45 minutes. When they feel slightly soft and tender to touch (remember, don't pierce them), they are done. Plunge them immediately into cold water. Once cool enough to handle, remove skins. Slice into desired thickness. Combine sugar, cornstarch, and vinegar in large saucepan. Bring mixture to boil and simmer 5 minutes. Add sliced beets and heat for a minute or so until beets are hot. Just before serving, sprinkle with "C" and add margarine.
Let margarine melt into sauce and serve.

Per Serving: about ½-¾ cup
Calories: 137
Fat: 3.8 gm
Cholesterol: 0 mg
Sodium: 87 mg
Carbohydrate: 23.9 gm
Protein: 1.1 gm

BROCCOLI WITH LEMON BUTTER

SERVES 6
248 mg vitamin C per serving • ☆ *Beta Carotene*

1 bunch fresh broccoli
2 tablespoons margarine
2 teaspoons lemon juice

¼ teaspoon salt
¼ teaspoon white pepper
¼ teaspoon "C"

Trim broccoli by removing yellow leaves and tough part of stalk. Wash it and pat dry. Steam broccoli 15 minutes or until tender.

Melt margarine and add lemon juice, salt, and pepper. Remove from heat and add "C" just before serving.
Note for dieters: You can simply steam broccoli and sprinkle "C" and lemon juice over top of hot vegetable, eliminating margarine.

Per Serving: ¾-1 cup
Calories: 56
Fat: 3.9 gm
Cholesterol: 0 mg
Sodium: 141 mg
Carbohydrate: 3.3 gm
Protein: 1.8 gm

BROCCOLI WITH BACON AND ONIONS

SERVES 6
248 mg vitamin C per serving • ☆ *Beta Carotene*

1 bunch fresh broccoli
3 strips bacon
⅓ cup bread crumbs
½ cup onions, finely chopped

3 tablespoons olive oil
1 clove garlic, mashed
¼ teaspoon "C"

Trim broccoli. Wash carefully. Steam until almost cooked, but not completely. Remove from pan. Cook bacon until lightly browned and drain on paper towels. When cool, crumble into small bits and set aside.
Sauté bread crumbs in bacon fat until lightly browned. Remove from pan and set aside. Using same pan, cook onions in olive oil 8 minutes or until transparent. Add garlic. Just before serving, add almost-cooked broccoli. Turn heat to medium and thoroughly heat vegetable. Add bread crumbs and bacon and lightly toss. Remove from heat and add "C." Serve immediately.

Per Serving: ¾-1 cup
Calories: 126
Fat: 8.7 gm
Cholesterol: 3 mg
Sodium: 126 mg
Carbohydrate: 8.1 gm
Protein: 3.6 gm

FRESH BROCCOLI WITH CHEESE SAUCE

SERVES 6
58 mg vitamin C per serving • ☆ Beta Carotene

**1 bunch fresh broccoli
(about 1½ lbs.)**
1 tablespoon margarine
2 tablespoons all-purpose flour
**1 teaspoon onion & herb
seasoning blend**

¼ teaspoon pepper
1½ cups skim milk
**1 cup shredded low-fat
taco or low-fat cheddar
cheese**

Wash broccoli, removing large leaves and tough parts of stalks. Separate into florets. Place broccoli in large saucepan with 1 inch boiling water. Cover. Cook 10-12 minutes, until just tender. Drain. Meanwhile, melt margarine in saucepan over medium heat. Stir in flour and seasonings; blend well. Add milk and cook, stirring constantly, until sauce thickens and comes to a boil. Add cheese; stir until cheese melts and sauce is smooth. Serve sauce over broccoli.

Per Serving: ½ cup
Calories: 149
Fat: 5.7 gm
Cholesterol: 14 mg
Sodium: 199 mg
Carbohydrate: 12. 5 gm
Protein: 11.8 gm

STIR-FRIED BROCCOLI

SERVES 4
58 mg vitamin C per serving • ☆ Beta Carotene

**1 bunch fresh broccoli
(about 1½ lbs.)**
1 tablespoon vegetable oil

**1 teaspoon onion & herb
seasoning or substitute**
**1 teaspoon oriental
blend seasoning**

Wash broccoli well. Cut off florets and cut stalks into 1-inch pieces.
Heat oil in large skillet. Add broccoli and seasonings; cook uncovered over

medium heat, stirring frequently, until broccoli is just tender, 7-10 minutes. Turn into heated serving dish.

Per Serving: about ½ cup
Calories: 79
Fat: 3.8 gm
Cholesterol: 0 mg
Sodium: 17 mg
Carbohydrate: 7 gm
Protein: 4.1 gm

BROCCOLI PARMIGIANA

SERVES 6
59 mg vitamin C per serving • ☆ Beta Carotene

1 bunch (1½ lbs.)	**1 tablespoon water**
fresh broccoli	**1 tablespoon olive oil**
1 tablespoon fresh	**¾ cup grated Parmesan**
lemon juice	**cheese**

Wash broccoli. Split all large stems to decrease cooking time. Place in saucepan with 1 inch water. Bring to boil and cook 5 minutes, uncovered. Cover and cook 5-10 minutes or until tender. Heat lemon juice, water, and olive oil in saucepan; pour over broccoli. Sprinkle with Parmesan cheese. Serve at once.

Per Serving: ½ cup
Calories: 114
Fat: 5.7 gm
Cholesterol: 8 gm
Sodium: 203 mg
Carbohydrate: 7.3 gm
Protein: 8.3 gm

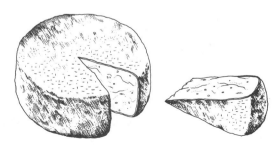

CREOLE BROCCOLI

SERVES 6
157 mg vitamin C per serving • ☆ *Beta Carotene*

¼ cup water + 2 teaspoons
  or 2 cubes low-sodium
  chicken broth granules
1 cup fresh tomatoes, diced
½ cup celery
¼ cup onions, chopped
½ cup green pepper, diced

¼ teaspoon hot sauce
⅛ teaspoon ground
  black pepper
1 bunch fresh broccoli
  (about 2 lbs.)
2 teaspoons cornstarch

To low-sodium broth, add tomatoes, celery, onion, green pepper, hot sauce, and pepper. Mix well. Wash and trim broccoli. Cut into spears. Place over vegetables (not in liquid). Cover tightly. Cook over medium heat until tender (15-20 minutes). Place broccoli on plates. Stir cornstarch into juice and vegetables. Cook until slightly thickened. Serve spoonful over each serving of broccoli, or pour thickened sauce over broccoli on serving dish.

Per Serving: about 1½ cups
Calories: 89
Fat: 0.8 gm
Cholesterol: 1 mg
Sodium: 59 mg
Carbohydrate: 13.9 gm
Protein: 6.5 gm

BRUSSELS SPROUTS PARMESAN

SERVES 6
200 mg vitamin C per serving

1 pound Brussels sprouts
2 small cloves garlic, chopped
2 tablespoons melted
  margarine
1 tablespoon lemon juice
¼ teaspoon "C"

¼ teaspoon salt
½ teaspoon freshly
  ground pepper
3 tablespoons grated low-
  fat Parmesan cheese

Remove any wilted outer leaves from sprouts and rinse sprouts under cold water to remove dirt particles. In saucepan steam for 10-15 minutes until just tender. Drain thoroughly. Return to saucepan. In small pan, sauté garlic in margarine until limp. Add lemon juice, "C," salt, and pepper. Pour over sprouts, and shake to coat. Spoon into serving dish and top with grated cheese.

Per Serving: 1-1¼ cups
Calories: 91
Fat: 4.8 gm
Cholesterol: 2 mg
Sodium: 183 mg
Carbohydrate: 7.0 gm
Protein: 4.9 gm

RED CABBAGE BRAISED WITH RED WINE AND APPLES

SERVES 8
152 mg vitamin C per serving

1 (3 lbs.) red cabbage, finely shredded
3 tablespoons corn oil margarine
¼ teaspoon salt
¼ teaspoon freshly ground pepper

1 cup dry red wine
2 tart apples, cored and diced (not peeled)
2 tablespoons brown sugar
¾ tablespoon vinegar
¼ teaspoon "C"

Remove outer leaves of cabbage and cut in half. Soak for a moment in cold water. Drain. Melt margarine in large skillet with lid. (Skillet should be enamel or Teflon, not aluminum or any other type of metal.) Add cabbage and toss to coat with margarine. When it begins to wilt, add salt, pepper, and red wine. Simmer 5 minutes. Add apples and sprinkle in brown sugar and vinegar. Cover skillet and simmer until apples and cabbage are tender— about 1 hour. Just before serving, taste for seasoning and sprinkle in "C." Toss to mix in "C," heat 1 minute, and serve.

Per Serving: 1½-2 cups
Calories: 148
Fat: 4.6 gm
Cholesterol: 0 mg
Sodium: 152 mg
Carbohydrate: 21.6 gm
Protein: 3.5 gm

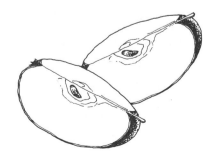

SOUR CREAM CABBAGE

SERVES 6
200 mg vitamin C per serving

½ **clove garlic, minced**
2 **tablespoons corn oil
margarine**
8 **cups firmly packed cabbage,
finely shredded**
¼ **cup boiling water**

⅓ **cup nonfat sour cream**
1½ **teaspoons lemon juice**
1 **tablespoon sugar**
¼ **teaspoon salt**
½ **teaspoon celery seed**
¼ **teaspoon "C"**

Sauté garlic in margarine in large skillet for several minutes. Add cabbage and water. Simmer 10 minutes or until tender. Add sour cream, lemon juice, sugar, salt, celery seed, and "C." Toss and serve.

Per Serving: about 1 cup
Calories: 84
Fat: 4.0 gm
Cholesterol: 0 mg
Sodium: 251 mg
Carbohydrate: 9.5 gm
Protein: 2.3 gm

CONFETTI CABBAGE

SERVES 6
32 mg vitamin C per serving • ☆ *Beta Carotene* • ☆ *E*

2 **tablespoons salad oil**
1 **onion, sliced**
2 **cloves garlic, minced**
6 **cups cabbage, thinly sliced**
2 **carrots, sliced**

1 **medium zucchini, cut
into julienne strips**
¼ **teaspoon salt**
½ **teaspoon caraway seed**

In 5-quart Dutch oven over high heat, cook onion and garlic in hot oil until onion is tender; stir frequently. Add remaining ingredients. Stirring quickly and frequently, cook cabbage until just tender, about 10 minutes.

Per Serving: about 1¹/₂ cups
Calories: 73
Fat: 3.8 gm
Cholesterol: 0 mg
Sodium: 86 mg
Carbohydrate: 7.7 gm
Protein: 1.8 gm

ONION AND CABBAGE SLAW

SERVES 8

22 mg vitamin C per serving • ☆ E

4 cups white cabbage, shredded	**2 tablespoons cider vinegar**
1 cup white onion rings	**6 tablespoons corn or sunflower oil**
½ cup parsley, chopped	**¼ teaspoon salt**
1 tablespoon caraway seeds	**¼ teaspoon white pepper**

Soak cabbage and onion together in water. Drain and dry and place in salad bowl. Sprinkle with parsley and caraway seeds, and toss lightly.

Combine vinegar, oil, salt, and pepper in small jar. Cover and shake well. Toss with vegetables. Cover and refrigerate 1-2 hours before serving.

Per Serving: about ½-⅔ cup
Calories: 117
Fat: 10.5 gm
Cholesterol: 0 mg
Sodium: 78 mg
Carbohydrate: 4.3 gm
Protein: 1.0 gm

CELERY IN WHITE WINE WITH TARRAGON

SERVES 6
170 mg vitamin C per serving

2 cups cut-up celery (thin
  match-size pieces)
1 cup Chicken Broth
  (recipe page 28)
1 teaspoon dried tarragon,
  tightly wrapped in
  cheesecloth
¼ cup dry white wine or
  vermouth (optional)

1 tablespoon corn oil
  margarine
1 tablespoon all-purpose
  flour
¼ teaspoon salt
¼ teaspoon pepper
¼ teaspoon "C"
Chopped fresh parsley

In saucepan, combine celery, Chicken Broth, and tarragon. Simmer slowly
until celery is just tender (about 5 minutes). Drain, and save cooking liquid.
Discard tarragon. Add enough white wine to cooking liquid to make a cup.
Bring it to boil. In small saucepan, melt margarine and add flour, stirring
constantly. Gradually add margarine and flour to liquid, stirring constantly.
When sauce begins to thicken, add salt and pepper to taste. Add celery and
reheat. Add "C." Sprinkle with chopped parsley.

Per Serving: ⅓-½ cup
Calories: 49
Fat: 2.0 gm
Cholesterol: trace
Sodium: 150 mg
Carbohydrate: 4.1 gm
Protein: 0.8 gm

BRAISED GREENS WITH HAM BITS

SERVES 6
200 mg vitamin C per serving   •   ☆ Beta Carotene

1 pound each collard greens,
  dandelions, mustard greens
1 cup chopped, cooked
  lean ham

1/16 teaspoon nutmeg
1 tablespoon vinegar
¼ teaspoon "C"
1 cup green onions, chopped

Wash greens and leave them damp. Place wet greens and cooked ham in large heavy saucepan. Steam until greens are wilted, about 25 minutes, tossing occasionally. Reduce heat and cook until tender. Add nutmeg, vinegar, "C," and green onions. Toss again and serve immediately.

Per Serving: 1½-2 cups
Calories: 156
Fat: 2.9 gm
Cholesterol: 13 mg
Sodium: 422 mg
Carbohydrate: 18.1 gm
Protein: 14.1 gm

STEAMED TURNIP GREENS WITH VINEGAR
SERVES 4
300 mg vitamin C per serving • ☆ *Beta Carotene*

2 pounds turnip greens
4 teaspoons melted margarine
¼ teaspoon salt

¼ teaspoon pepper
¼ teaspoon "C"
Cruet of white vinegar

Wash greens and leave damp. Discard any brown or wilted leaves.
Steam greens until they wilt, approximately 15-20 minutes. Shake pan occasionally so greens will not stick to bottom. Drain well and chop them into bite-sized pieces.
Add margarine, salt, pepper, and "C." Serve with a cruet of vinegar.

Per Serving: about 1½ cups
Calories: 113
Fat: 4.4 gm
Cholesterol: 0 mg
Sodium: 223 mg
Carbohydrate: 11.4 gm
Protein: 6.8 gm

BRAISED KALE LEAVES

SERVES 6

228 mg vitamin C per serving • ☆ *Beta Carotene*

2 pounds kale
½ cup Beef Broth
  (recipe page 26)
¼ teaspoon salt
1 tablespoon corn oil
  margarine

¼ teaspoon "C"
¼ teaspoon nutmeg,
  freshly grated

Wash kale carefully. Pat dry and cut leaves off stems. Heat Beef Broth in large saucepan and add kale. Simmer until tender, 8-10 minutes. Drain. Season with salt. Stir in margarine, "C," and nutmeg. Serve.

Per Serving: about 2 cups
Calories: 121
Fat: 3.1 gm
Cholesterol: trace
Sodium: 297 mg
Carbohydrate: 14.0 gm
Protein: 9.2 gm

BRAISED SPINACH

SERVES 6

180 mg vitamin C per serving • ☆ *Beta Carotene*

2 pounds fresh spinach
2 tablespoons corn oil
  margarine
2 tablespoons lemon juice
¼ teaspoon salt

¼ teaspoon pepper
¼ teaspoon "C"
1/16 teaspoon nutmeg,
  freshly grated

Wash spinach very carefully to get rid of sand and dirt. Trim off stems and any discolored leaves. Do not pat dry. Melt margarine in large, deep-sided saucepan (one large enough to accommodate all spinach at outset—it will decrease in volume the moment it begins to cook). Add lemon juice, salt, pepper, and spinach; cook quickly. It will take just a few minutes until spinach is wilted and limp. Continue cooking for another minute to make sure stalks are tender. Add "C" and correct seasoning. Garnish with a little freshly grated nutmeg.

Per Serving: about 1 cup
Calories: 86
Fat: 4.2 gm
Cholesterol: 0 mg
Sodium: 233 mg
Carbohydrate: 7.0 gm
Protein: 4.9 gm

SPINACH IN MADEIRA
SERVES 6
180 mg vitamin C per serving • ☆ *Beta Carotene*

2 pounds fresh spinach
2 tablespoons corn oil margarine
¼ cup evaporated skim milk
¼ teaspoon salt
¼ teaspoon pepper

¹⁄₁₆ teaspoon nutmeg, freshly grated
¼ pound fresh mushrooms, thinly sliced
3 tablespoons Madeira wine
¼ teaspoon "C"

Wash spinach carefully. Remove wilted leaves. Steam quickly in large saucepan, using only water remaining on leaves after washing.
Toss constantly until spinach is just tender, about 5 minutes.
Put spinach through finest blade on food processor. Add margarine and skim milk and mix thoroughly. Season with salt, pepper, and nutmeg. Set aside. Sauté mushrooms. Add mushrooms to spinach, along with Madeira. Reheat for few minutes, stir in "C," and serve.

Per Serving: about 1 cup
Calories: 109
Fat: 4.3 gm
Cholesterol: trace
Sodium: 247 mg
Carbohydrate: 9.2 gm
Protein: 6.2 gm

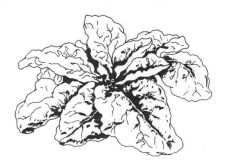

MINTED GREEN PEAS

SERVES 8

180 mg vitamin C per serving

3 pounds fresh peas
2 tablespoons corn oil
  margarine
¼ teaspoon salt

¼ teaspoon pepper
¼ teaspoon "C"
1½ tablespoons mint
  leaves, chopped

Shell peas. Place in heavy saucepan with lid, and add margarine and 3 table-spoons water. Cook slowly 20-25 minutes.

When peas are tender, season with salt, pepper, "C," and chopped mint leaves.

Per Serving: about 1 cup
Calories: 173
Fat: 3.4 gm
Cholesterol: 0 mg
Sodium: 98 mg
Carbohydrate: 24.5 gm
Protein: 10.7 gm

CREAMY BASIL POTATOES

SERVES 6

190 mg vitamin C per serving

2 pounds boiling potatoes
3 tablespoons corn oil
  margarine
1½ tablespoons all-purpose
  flour
1½ cups hot skim milk
¾ cup evaporated skim milk
1 tablespoon fresh basil or
  ½ teaspoon dried basil

1-2 large cloves garlic,
  mashed
¼ teaspoon salt
¼ teaspoon pepper
3 tablespoons fresh parsley,
  minced
¼ teaspoon "C"

Scrub potatoes thoroughly. Cut into ¼-inch slices. (If you must, you can peel them first—but remember you will be sacrificing valuable vitamin C and added taste.)

Steam 5 minutes. Remove potatoes from steamer and set aside.

Melt margarine in large saucepan. When margarine is bubbling but not brown, add flour. Mix with wire whisk and cook 2 minutes. Remove mixture from heat, and when it has stopped bubbling, add hot milk. Stir constantly until mixture is smooth. Blend in evaporated skim milk, basil, garlic, salt, and pepper. Simmer for a couple of minutes and then add potatoes. If sauce does not cover potatoes, add a little more milk. Cook very slowly for 10-15 minutes until potatoes are tender. Stir occasionally to prevent them from sticking.

Just before serving, add minced parsley, "C," and any correct seasoning. Serve at once.

Note: Tarragon can be substituted for basil, if desired.

Per Serving: 1-1¼ cups
Calories: 218
Fat: 5.9 gm
Cholesterol: 2 mg
Sodium: 215 mg
Carbohydrate: 33.3 gm
Protein: 7.9 gm

MARINATED ZUCCHINI

SERVES 6
170 mg vitamin C per serving • ☆ E

6 small zucchini
2 teaspoons prepared mustard
¼ teaspoon salt
¼ teaspoon pepper
2 teaspoons vinegar

¼ teaspoon "C"
½ clove garlic, minced
½ cup corn oil
Sugar to taste

Wash any dirt particles off zucchini. Pat dry with paper towels. Cut zucchini into thin slices and steam 2-3 minutes until just tender, but still crunchy. Cool. Prepare marinade by shaking remaining ingredients together in jar. When zucchini have cooled, place into bowl along with marinade. Refrigerate for several hours and serve chilled.

If you like, garnish zucchini with sliced cherry tomatoes.

Per Serving: about 1 cup
Calories: 176
Fat: 18.4 gm
Cholesterol: 0 mg
Sodium: 85 mg
Carbohydrate: 3.8 gm
Protein: 1.4 gm

ZUCCHINI IN SOUR CREAM
SERVES 6
335 mg vitamin C per serving

6 small zucchini
2 tablespoons corn oil
margarine
2 tablespoons nonfat
sour cream

½ teaspoon "C"
¼ teaspoon pepper
¼ teaspoon salt

Wash off any dirt from zucchini and pat dry. Do not peel. Cut into thin slices. Melt margarine in large skillet and toss in zucchini. Cook until just tender, 2-3 minutes, but still crunchy—the best way to tell, of course, is to sample as you cook; it will take just a few minutes to cook them.
Add sour cream, "C," salt, and pepper and toss until zucchini are well coated with sour cream. Serve.
Note: We recommend small zucchini because they have a much better flavor than larger ones.

Per Serving: about ¾-1 cup
Calories: 56
Fat: 3.8 gm
Cholesterol: 0 mg
Sodium: 135 mg
Carbohydrate: 3.7 gm
Protein: 1.6 gm

ZUCCHINI STIR-FRY
SERVES 5
121 mg vitamin C per serving • ☆ Beta Carotene • ☆ E

½ pound zucchini, sliced
½ pound yellow squash, cut
in pieces
½ pound broccoli florets
½ pound cauliflower florets
½ pound snow peas

½ cup sesame oil
1 tablespoon garlic
½ teaspoon ginger, freshly
grated
1 pimiento, chopped and
squeezed

Bring large pot of water to boil. Blanch each of first five ingredients separately for 1 minute. Drain each and place immediately in ice water. Heat oil in pan until hot. Add garlic and ginger and sauté for 1 minute and 30 seconds. Add vegetables and toss ingredients until hot. Add chopped pimiento.

Per Serving: about 2 cups
Calories: 289
Fat: 22.9 gm
Cholesterol: 0 mg
Sodium: 20 mg
Carbohydrate: 14.9 gm
Protein: 5.6 gm

ORANGE-PECAN SWEET POTATOES

SERVES 8
30 mg vitamin C per serving • ☆ Beta Carotene • ☆ E

2 pounds sweet potatoes, pared, cut into scant ½" slices
¼ cup orange juice
⅓ cup packed light-brown sugar

¼ teaspoon ground cinnamon
¼ teaspoon ground nutmeg
¼ cup corn oil margarine
¼ cup pecans, coarsely chopped

Place sweet potatoes and orange juice in 1½-quart microwaveable casserole; cover with microwave wrap and vent one edge. Microwave on High 6 minutes. Stir in brown sugar, cinnamon, and nutmeg; dot with margarine. Microwave, covered, on High 6 minutes; stir after 3 minutes. Microwave, uncovered, 1 minute; stir. Sprinkle pecans over potatoes; microwave, uncovered, 1 minute.

Per Serving: ½-¾ cup
Calories: 211
Fat: 8.3 gm
Cholesterol: 0 mg
Sodium: 63 mg
Carbohydrate: 32.0 gm
Protein: 1.7 gm

DEEP DISH YAMS

SERVES 6
19 mg vitamin C per serving • ☆ *Beta Carotene* • ☆ *E*

5 tablespoons corn oil
margarine
1 medium onion
3 cups boiled yams, peeled
and sliced
2 cups apple chunks

½ cup celery, diced
¾ cup brown sugar
1 teaspoon lemon juice
1 teaspoon dried basil
¼ teaspoon white pepper
2 tablespoons rum (optional)

Preheat oven to 350° F.
Sauté onion in 2 tablespoons margarine until tender; set aside. Melt remaining margarine in small saucepan. Grease deep 8-inch baking dish and layer with yams. Cover with some apple chunks and celery and sprinkle with a little onion, one-half of brown sugar, lemon juice, basil, pepper, and melted margarine. Repeat process using rest of ingredients and finish with layer of apples and brown sugar. Sprinkle with lemon juice and rum, if desired. Bake, uncovered, 30 minutes.

Per Serving: about 1 cup
Calories: 296
Fat: 0.3 gm
Cholesterol: 0 mg
Sodium: 110 mg
Carbohydrate: 49.7 gm
Protein: 1.5 gm

SOUFFLÉ STUFFED SWEET POTATOES

SERVES 12
14 mg vitamin C per serving • ☆ *Beta Carotene* • ☆ *E*

6 small sweet potatoes
2 eggs, separated
1 teaspoon allspice
1 cup low-fat milk

¼ teaspoon cream of tartar
½ cup raisins
½ cup toasted pecans

Prick sweet potatoes several times with fork. Place in microwave on paper towel. Microwave on High until potatoes are tender (15-18 minutes); turn potatoes once during cooking. When cool enough to handle, cut potatoes in half lengthwise. Scoop out centers and leave ¼-inch shell. Combine potato, egg yolks, and allspice in mixing bowl; beat until smooth; add milk gradually; set aside. In a separate mixing bowl; beat egg whites and cream of tartar to form soft peaks. Fold egg whites and raisins into potato mixture. Spoon soufflé mixture into each potato shell. Top each potato with pecans. Place stuffed potatoes on serving platter. Cover with plastic wrap. Potatoes can be refrigerated up to 1 day before serving. Just before serving, microwave stuffed potatoes on High until heated through (9-11 minutes).

Per Serving: 1 stuffed potato half
Calories: 152
Fat: 4.8 gm
Cholesterol: 37 mg
Sodium: 31 mg
Carbohydrate: 23.4 gm
Protein: 3.4 gm

NUTTY SWEET POTATOES
SERVES 4
42 mg vitamin C per serving • ☆ Beta Carotene • ☆ E

4 sweet potatoes (or yams)
6 tablespoons corn oil margarine
4 tablespoons sherry
½ cup orange juice
¼ teaspoon nutmeg

1 cup pecans, chopped
¼ teaspoon salt
¼ teaspoon pepper
1 tablespoon brown sugar
½ teaspoon cinnamon

Choose potatoes of uniform size and shape. Scrub well and pierce twice through with fork or skewer. Place in a circle on paper towel and bake in microwave oven 16-18 minutes. Potatoes should be tender when tested with a fork. Remove from oven; let stand 5 minutes. Peel potatoes, and slice into electric mixing bowl. Beat potatoes with margarine, sherry, orange juice, and nutmeg until smooth. Stir in pecans and season to taste with salt and pepper. Place mixture into microwave-safe serving dish. Combine brown sugar, cinnamon, and sprinkle on top. Microwave, uncovered, on High 4 minutes, turning dish 90 degrees after 2 minutes. Serve.

Per Serving: about 1 cup
Calories: 547
Fat: 37.1 gm
Cholesterol: 0 mg
Sodium: 306 mg
Carbohydrate: 44.6 gm
Protein: 4.6 gm

PERFECT GARLIC MASHED POTATOES

SERVES 4
26 mg vitamin C per serving • ☆ E

1½ pounds (4 medium)
  potatoes
1 cup low-fat milk
2 tablespoons 100% corn oil
  margarine

3 cloves garlic, minced
½ teaspoon salt
½ teaspoon pepper
Chopped parsley, for
  garnish

In microwave, cook potatoes on High 13 minutes. Halve potatoes lengthwise; scoop out pulp into medium microwave-safe bowl. Mash potatoes with potato masher, or beat with electric hand mixer; set aside. Place milk, margarine, and garlic in small microwave-safe bowl. Microwave on High 2 minutes. Thoroughly mix into potato pulp. If necessary, add more milk to reach creamier consistency. Season with salt and pepper. Cook in microwave on High 1 minute. Serve immediately. Garnish with parsley, if desired.

Per Serving: about ½ cup
Calories: 169
Fat: 6.2 gm
Cholesterol: 3 mg
Sodium: 345 mg
Carbohydrates: 24.2 gm
Protein: 3.9 gm

FLOWERED CHILLED PASTA

SERVES 4
63 mg vitamin C per serving • ☆ Beta Carotene • ☆ E

1 pound wheat pasta
½ pound handmade zucchini
  florets or simple slices
½ pound handmade carrot
  florets or simple slices
½ pound yellow squash

¼ pound broccoli florets
¼ pound cauliflower florets
½ pound shiitake
  mushrooms
1 tablespoon garlic
¼ cup corn oil

Cook pasta in salted water *al dente*. Rinse in cold water. Blanch zucchini, carrots, and squash 1-2 minutes. Blanch broccoli and cauliflower 2-3 minutes, leaving slightly crisp. Set broccoli only in bath of ice water to hold color. Sauté shiitake mushrooms in oil with garlic. Toss pasta and vegetables together, reserving 3 of each for top garnish.

Per Serving: about 3 cups
Calories: 639
Fat: 16.3 gm
Cholesterol: 0 mg
Sodium: 51 mg
Carbohydrate: 102.7 gm
Protein: 19.6 gm

VEGETARIAN WHEAT-GERM TOSTADO

SERVES 4
35 mg vitamin C per serving • ☆ E

4 tortillas
2 medium tomatoes, diced
1½ cups low-fat Monterey Jack cheese, grated
¾ cup regular wheat germ
1 can (7-7½ oz.) green chili sauce
½ cup celery, sliced
⅓ cup green onion, chopped
2 tablespoons tomato sauce
4 cups lettuce, torn
1 avocado, peeled, pitted and mashed
2 teaspoons lemon juice
½ cup plain low-fat yogurt

Place tortillas in single layer on baking sheet. Bake at 350° F. for 10 minutes, or until crisp. Combine tomatoes, cheese, wheat germ, chili sauce, celery, onion, and tomato sauce. Mix well. Place tortillas on serving plates. Top with lettuce. Spread wheat-germ mixture onto lettuce. Combine mashed avocado and lemon juice. Spoon onto wheat-germ mixture. Top with yogurt. Sprinkle with additional wheat germ, if desired.

Per Serving: 1 filled tortilla
Calories: 421
Fat: 18.5 gm
Cholesterol: 25 mg
Sodium: 422 mg
Carbohydrate: 42.7 gm
Protein: 20.6 gm

CARROTS WITH DILL

SERVES 6
170 mg vitamin C per serving • ☆ Beta Carotene

12 medium-sized carrots
3 tablespoons corn oil
  margarine
¼ teaspoon salt
½ teaspoon freshly ground
  pepper

¼ teaspoon "C"
1 tablespoon chopped
  fresh dill or 1½
  teaspoons dried dill

Scrub carrots and slice into thin pieces. If you like, remove peel instead of scrubbing. Steam carrot slices until tender, approximately 8-10 minutes. Melt margarine in skillet and add carrots. Shake pan until slices are well coated with margarine. Add salt, pepper, "C," and dill. Toss to blend in seasonings and serve.

Per Serving: about 1-1¼ cups
Calories: 118
Fat: 5.8 gm
Cholesterol: 0 mg
Sodium: 146 mg
Carbohydrate: 14.8 gm
Protein: 1.5 gm

CARROTS VICHY

SERVES 6
170 mg vitamin C per serving • ☆ Beta Carotene

1½ pounds carrots, peeled and
  cut into 2" pieces
2 tablespoons corn oil
  margarine

¼ teaspoon white pepper
¼ teaspoon "C"
4 tablespoons fresh
  parsley, chopped

Place carrots, margarine, and 3 tablespoons water in heavy saucepan with tight-fitting lid. Simmer for 30-40 minutes or until carrots are tender. While they are cooking, shake pan occasionally to move carrots around and keep them from sticking to pan.

Season with pepper and "C." Toss carrots carefully with chopped parsley and serve.

Per Serving: about 1 cup
Calories: 93
Fat: 3.9 gm
Cholesterol: 0 mg
Sodium: 87 mg
Carbohydrate: 11.3 gm
Protein: 1.3 gm

CARROTS CARIBBEAN-STYLE

MAKES 1⅔ CUPS (3 SERVINGS)
15 mg vitamin C per serving • ☆ Beta Carotene

2 cups fresh carrots cut in julienne strips
¾ cup pineapple juice
¾ teaspoon ground cinnamon
⅛ teaspoon ground nutmeg
1/16 teaspoon ground black pepper

In medium saucepan, combine carrots, pineapple juice, cinnamon, nutmeg, and black pepper. Bring to boil. Reduce heat and simmer, covered, until carrots are just tender, about 15 minutes.

Per Serving: ½ cup
Calories: 67
Fat: 0.2 grams
Cholesterol: 0 mg
Sodium: 28 mg
Carbohydrates: 15.3 gm
Protein: 0.8 gm

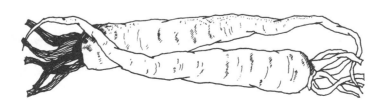

MARINATED CARROTS (MERRY CAROTENE)

SERVES 8
28 mg vitamin C per serving   •   ☆ Beta Carotene

**2 pounds carrots, cooked
  (do not overcook)**

Marinade:
**1 can tomato soup
1½ teaspoons hot pepper sauce
¼ cup oil
½ cup honey**

**1 medium bell pepper,
  sliced or slivered raw
1 medium onion, sliced**

**¾ cup apple-cider vinegar
1 teaspoon dry mustard
  (or 1 teaspoon prepared
  mustard)**

Mix marinade ingredients well. Drop onion and pepper slices into marinade. Pour marinade over drained, slightly cooked, and sliced carrots. Place in refrigerator. Store and chill 8-12 hours before serving. Will keep up to three weeks in refrigerator (if you can keep them that long).
Suggestions for gift-giving: Fill pint jars with these; top with lid. Type or print gummed label for side of jar identifying these as *"Merry Carotene"—must be refrigerated.* You could also fit the jar into a basket. Wrap, tag, and give to someone who appreciates something tangy. Makes a lovely hostess gift if you are going to a party.

Per Serving: ½ cup
Calories: 223
Fat: 7.9 grams
Cholesterol: 0 mg
Sodium: 259 mg
Carbohydrates: 34.8 gm
Protein: 2.1 gm

ITALIAN MARINATED CARROTS

MAKES 3 CUPS
about 7 mg vitamin C per serving   •   ☆ Beta Carotene

**1 pound carrots, peeled and
  cut into ½" slices
  (about 3½ cups)**

**2 teaspoons instant minced
  garlic
½ teaspoon salt**

½ cup olive oil
¼ cup red wine vinegar
1 tablespoon oregano

½ teaspoon ground black
    pepper

In medium saucepan, bring ½ cup salted water to boil. Add carrots. Return to boil. Reduce heat and simmer covered until carrots are just tender, about 10 minutes. Drain off liquid. In 1-quart jar, combine oil, vinegar, oregano, garlic, salt, and black pepper. Add drained carrots; mix well. Cover and refrigerate 24 hours, shaking jar at least once.

Per Serving: ½ cup
Calories: 212
Fat: 18.9 grams
Cholesterol: 0 mg
Sodium: 221 mg
Carbohydrates: 8.6 gm
Protein: 1.0 gm

CRUNCHY MARINATED CARROTS AND TURNIPS

SERVES 4
20mg vitamin C per serving • ☆ Beta Carotene

4 carrots, grated
1 large turnip, peeled and
    diced
1 tablespoon apple-cider
    vinegar

1 tablespoon vegetable oil
1 tablespoon orange juice
1 tablespoon Dijon mustard
1 teaspoon dried tarragon
1 teaspoon dried basil

In serving dish, combine carrots and turnips. In a separate bowl, combine remaining ingredients and pour over vegetables. Cover and refrigerate several hours before serving.

Per Serving: ¾ cup
Calories: 86
Fat: 4.5 gm
Cholesterol: 0 mg
Sodium: 163 mg
Carbohydrate: 1.2 gm
Protein: 1.0 gm

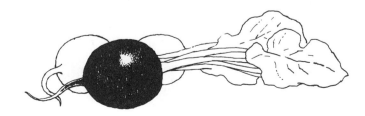

ITALIAN BROCCOLI WITH TOMATOES

SERVES 4
93 mg vitamin C per serving • ☆ *Beta Carotene*

4 cups fresh broccoli florets
½ cup water
½ teaspoon oregano leaves
⅛ teaspoon pepper

2 medium tomatoes, cut into wedges
½ cup low-fat mozzarella cheese, shredded

Place broccoli and water in 2-quart casserole; cover. Microwave on High, 5-8 minutes or until just tender. Drain. Stir in seasonings and tomatoes. Microwave, uncovered, on High, 2-4 minutes or until tomatoes are hot. Sprinkle with mozzarella. Microwave 1 minute or until cheese melts.

Per Serving: about 1½ cups
Calories: 60
Fat: 0.6 gm
Cholesterol: 8 mg
Sodium: 130 mg
Carbohydrate: 9.5 gm
Protein: 3.6 gm

EGGPLANT FLORENTINE

SERVES 6
7 mg vitamin C per serving • ☆ *Beta Carotene* • ☆ *E*

1 large eggplant (about 1 lb.)
2 tablespoons corn oil margarine, melted
1 (10-12 oz.) package frozen chopped spinach
1 (10½ oz.) can white sauce

½ cup blanched slivered almonds, toasted
⅛ teaspoon pepper
⅛ teaspoon nutmeg
¼ teaspoon garlic powder
3 tablespoons low-fat Parmesan cheese

Preheat oven to 400° F.
Wash and pare eggplant; cut crosswise into ½-inch slices. Brush melted margarine lightly on each side. Place on rimmed baking sheet and bake 10-12

minutes or until tender. Meanwhile, cook spinach according to package directions; drain and squeeze out water; mix with white sauce, almonds, and seasonings. Spoon onto baked eggplant slices; sprinkle with cheese or crumbs. Broil 2-3 minutes or until cheese is browned.

Per Serving: 1¼ cups
Calories: 211
Fat: 13.0 gm
Cholesterol: 2 mg
Sodium: 367 mg
Carbohydrate: 10.9 gm
Protein: 8.1 gm

ALMOND RICE CASSEROLE
SERVES 6
12 mg vitamin C per serving • ☆ Beta Carotene • ☆ E

4 tablespoons corn oil, divided
¾ cup blanched slivered almonds
1 cup diced carrots
1 cup diced celery
½ cup sliced green onion
½ cup diced green pepper

1 bay leaf
2 cups Chicken Broth (recipe page 28)
2 tablespoons reduced-sodium soy sauce
1 cup long-grain brown rice

Preheat oven to 350° F.
Heat 2 tablespoons oil in large skillet. Add almonds; sauté, stirring 2-3 minutes or until lightly toasted. Remove with slotted spoon. Add remaining oil and heat. Add all vegetables and bay leaf; stir over medium heat for several minutes. Pour into 1½-quart casserole; add Chicken Broth, soy sauce, and rice; stir. Cover and bake 70-80 minutes or until rice is tender and liquid is absorbed. Remove bay leaf. Stir in almonds and serve immediately.

Per Serving: 1-1¼ cups
Calories: 286
Fat: 18.5 gm
Cholesterol: 1 mg
Sodium: 142 mg
Carbohydrate: 23.2 gm
Protein: 6.4 gm

VEGETARIAN QUICHE

SERVES 6

35 mg vitamin C per serving   •   ☆ E

Crust:

1 cup whole-wheat flour
¼ teaspoon salt

⅓ cup corn oil
3 tablespoons low-fat milk

Filling:

1 cup broccoli, sliced
1 cup cauliflower, sliced
3 tablespoons corn oil
½ green pepper, chopped
1 onion, chopped

1 cup low-fat milk
3 eggs, beaten
¾ cup low-fat mozarella
   cheese, grated

Preheat oven to 350° F.

Combine ingredients for crust (measure liquids together in ½-cup measure). Using hands, press small amounts of dough into deep pie plate until lined with pastry. Prick pastry and set aside.

Prepare vegetables: Cut broccoli and cauliflower into thin slices. Heat oil in heavy skillet, and sauté onion and green pepper 1-2 minutes. Add broccoli and cauliflower, and stir-fry until just tender.

In bowl combine milk, eggs, and cheese. Add vegetables, removing them from skillet with slotted spoon. Pour into crust and bake 45 minutes or until set.

Per Serving: ⅙ pie
Calories: 370
Fat: 25.5 gm
Cholesterol: 118 mg
Sodium: 257 mg
Carbohydrate: 22.1 gm
Protein: 12.8 gm

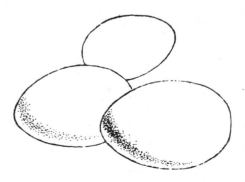

RISI-BISI CASSEROLE

SERVES 4

6 mg vitamin C per serving • ☆ E

¼ **teaspoon salt**
½ **cup rice**
½ **cup onion, chopped**
¼ **cup corn oil margarine**
1 **package (10 oz.) frozen peas**
1 **teaspoon basil, crushed**
½ **teaspoon thyme, crushed**

¼ **teaspoon rosemary,**
  crushed
1½ **cups slivered almonds,**
  toasted, divided
2 **cups low-fat cheddar,**
  grated, divided

Preheat oven to 375° F.
In large saucepan, bring 1 cup water to boil. Add salt, rice, and onion. Cover and cook over very low heat 20 minutes or until rice is just tender. Stir in margarine, peas, basil, thyme, rosemary, 1 cup almonds, and 1 cup cheese. Heat thoroughly. Turn into 1½-quart baking dish. Top with remaining cheese and almonds. Bake 25 minutes or until hot in center.

Per Serving: about 1 cup
Calories: 450
Fat: 48.0 gm
Cholesterol: 40 mg
Sodium: 688 mg
Carbohydrate: 28.9 gm
Protein: 31.5 gm

Salads

The salad story is a very popular one today. The public is becoming increasingly aware of a proper balance in diet. Particularly at lunch, the salad has come into its own as a substitute for the heavy, although tempting, meat dish that puts weight on eyelids later in the afternoon and weight on waistline later in the week.

Salads are particularly attractive visually, and there are many designs in bowls and plates that lend a great flourish to this fairly simple dish.

Whether you serve salads before, with, or after the main course, they can provide a nourishing, high "C" contrast in taste and texture as well as visual appeal. To ensure crisp and exquisitely delicate texture, both the salad bowl and serving plates should be chilled in the freezer.

Basic Green Salad

The most popular salad is the tossed mixed greens. It can be a thing of beauty and high in vitamin C, provided the greens are fresh and you take a little trouble. The amount of vitamin C will be determined by your selection of ingredients. To calculate the amount of vitamin C per serving, refer to the Appendix.

Once home with the greens, separate the leaves, remove any stem or core, and wash the leaves thoroughly but quickly in cold water. Dry the leaves by using cloth or paper towels, or use a salad spinner.

There are three reasons for drying the greens. One is to retain as much vitamin C as possible. Another is that oil will not adhere to the greens if they are wet. Third, wet greens become soggy instead of crisp.

Once you have dried the greens, refrigerate them in a plastic bag, removing as much air as possible from the bag before sealing, until you are ready to use them.

The simplest way of dressing the salad is to put 3 or 4 tablespoons of oil in the bottom of a chilled bowl. (You may use any oil you like: olive, peanut, soybean, grape seed, corn, vegetable, or a combination.) Add ¼ teaspoon dry mustard, ⅛ teaspoon "C," and 1 tablespoon lemon juice. Mix thoroughly with a fork. If you wish, you may rub the bowl with a clove of garlic. Place greens in the bowl. Use various kinds of lettuce, watercress, spinach, mustard greens, and dandelion greens. Toss the greens with a large fork and spoon, preferably wooden, lifting the leaves into the air, then dropping and picking up another batch until they are completely coated with oil.

To this basic green salad you may add whatever seems pleasing— mushrooms, zucchini, radishes, onions, green pepper, tomato, and cucumbers. Canned mandarin oranges (chilled and drained) or fresh orange and/or grapefruit sections are a pleasant contrast to tossed greens.

You may want to add cheese, such as blue, Roquefort, or Swiss. Feta is another popular cheese you may wish to try, if you can find it—a salty, white Greek cheese, made of goat's milk.

Hard-boiled eggs, tuna, and olives are other possibilities, as are cubes of leftover beef, pork, ham, chicken.

If using sliced avocado, add it last, sprinkled with "C" dissolved in water or lemon juice. This will keep the avocado from turning brown.

Store any leftover salad in an air-tight zip-top plastic bag to be used later for Vegetable Broth (recipe page 27). Many cookbooks advise never to wash a wooden salad bowl, but simply to wipe it clean. However, the oil in the bowl eventually turns rancid and in no way enhances future salads—so *do* wash wooden salad bowls.

TOMATOES STUFFED WITH PESTO

SERVES 6
240 mg vitamin C per serving • ☆ E

**6 medium, firm, ripe
tomatoes**

**1 recipe Pesto Sauce (below)
6 leaves Boston lettuce**

Peel tomatoes and remove seeds. Turn tomatoes upside down on paper towels and drain. Fill tomatoes with Pesto Sauce and serve on a leaf of lettuce.

Per Serving: 1 filled tomato
Calories: 362
Fat: 38.1 gm
Cholesterol: 6 mg
Sodium: 215 mg
Carbohydrate: 7.7 gm
Protein: 5.7 gm

PESTO SAUCE

SERVES 6 (MAKES 1¼ CUPS)
200 mg vitamin C per serving • ☆ E

**2 cups fresh Italian (flat leaf)
parsley or fresh basil leaves
torn into small pieces**
¾ cup olive oil
2 tablespoons pine nuts

1 teaspoon garlic, chopped
¼ teaspoon "C",
**½ cup low-fat Parmesan
cheese, freshly grated**
3 tablespoons soft margarine

Place parsley, olive oil, pine nuts, and garlic into blender and process on high speed. Stop occasionally to scrape down sides.
When ingredients are well blended, pour into bowl and beat in "C" and cheese by hand. Stir in softened margarine.
This sauce is traditionally used for spaghetti or linguine.

Per Serving: about 3 tablespoons
Calories: 366
Fat: 37.7 gm
Cholesterol: 6 mg
Sodium: 203 mg
Carbohydrate: 1.8 gm
Protein: 4.6 gm

WHEAT-GERM STUFFED TOMATO SALAD

SERVES 4
34 mg vitamin C per serving   •   ☆ E

1 whole chicken breast,
  boned, skinned, and diced
1 teaspoon corn oil
  margarine
4 large firm, ripe tomatoes
¾ cup wheat germ
⅓ cup green onion, chopped

⅓ cup green pepper, chopped
¾ teaspoon dillweed
½ teaspoon thyme leaves,
  crushed
⅛ teaspoon cayenne pepper
Avocado wedges
Ripe olives

Sauté chicken in margarine until tender (about 5 minutes). Cut thin slice from tops of tomatoes. Scoop out pulp, leaving shells intact. Dice tomato tops with pulp. Drain. Combine all ingredients, except tomato shells. Mix well. Spoon mixture into shells. Serve on lettuce garnished with avocado wedges and ripe olives, if desired. To serve hot, place in shallow baking dish and bake at 350° F for about 25 minutes.

Per Serving: 1 tomato with ⅔ cup stuffing
Calories: 176
Fat: 4.9 gm
Cholesterol: 24 mg
Sodium: 37 mg
Carbohydrate: 17.9 gm
Protein: 15.1 gm

TOMATO AND CUCUMBER PLATE

SERVES 6
200 mg vitamin C per serving

4 ripe tomatoes, peeled
  and diced
2 large cucumbers, peeled,
  seeded, and thinly sliced
½ Bermuda onion, thinly
  sliced in rings

2 tablespoons corn oil
1 tablespoon lemon juice
¼ teaspoon dry mustard
2 tablespoons fresh
  parsley, minced
¼ teapoon "C"

Arrange tomatoes, cucumbers, and onion rings on a large, attractive serving platter.

Combine oil, lemon juice, mustard, and parsley thoroughly. (Easiest way is to put in small jar, cover, and shake.) Chill. When ready to serve, add "C" to dressing, shake lightly, and pour over vegetables.

The taste of this salad depends a great deal upon quality of tomatoes and is best when prepared with garden-fresh, eating tomatoes.

Per Serving: 1¼-1½ cups
Calories: 92
Fat: 5.0 gm
Cholesterol: 0 mg
Sodium: 15 mg
Carbohydrate: 9.9 gm
Protein: 1.9 gm

SUMMER SPECIAL SALAD

SERVES 4
27 mg vitamin C per serving • ☆ Beta Carotene • ☆ E

1 Vidalia onion, thinly sliced
4 tomatoes, sliced
¼ cup canola or sunflower oil
1 tablespoon lemon juice

½ teaspoon minced garlic
¼ teaspoon salt
½ teaspoon oregano
** leaves**

Marinate onions and tomatoes with mixture of oil, juice, garlic, salt, and oregano at least 3 hours. Serve chilled.

Per Serving: about 1½ cups
Calories: 180
Fat: 14.1 gm
Cholesterol: 0 mg
Sodium: 150 mg
Carbohydrate: 11.6 gm
Protein: 1.8 gm

ONION, TOMATO, AND CUCUMBER SALAD IN ITALIAN DRESSING

SERVES 6

30 mg vitamin C per serving   •   ☆ *Beta Carotene*   •   ☆ *E*

1 Vidalia onion, sliced
6 tomatoes, peeled and sliced

2 large cucumbers, sliced
¼ cup Italian dressing (bottled)

Combine all vegetables in salad bowl. Add Italian dressing of personal choice. Refrigerate until ready to serve.

Per Serving: 1½-2 cups
Calories: 105
Fat: 4.6 gm
Cholesterol: 0 mg
Sodium: 95 mg
Carbohydrate: 13.2 gm
Protein: 2.4 gm

CUCUMBER SALAD

SERVES 4

260 mg vitamin C per serving

¾ cup nonfat sour cream
¼ teaspoon salt
¼ teaspoon freshly ground pepper
2 teaspoons vinegar
2 tablespoons fresh dill or
1 teaspoon dried dill

2 medium cucumbers, peeled, seeded, and thinly sliced
¼ teaspoon "C"

In bowl, combine sour cream, salt, pepper, vinegar, and dill. Add cucumber slices and toss until all slices are coated with sour cream dressing. Refrigerate until ready to serve. Mix in "C" just before serving.
Note: This is especially nice with fish.

Per Serving: about 1 cup
Calories: 69
Fat: 0.4 gm
Cholesterol: 1 mg
Sodium: 205 mg
Carbohydrate: 11.7 gm
Protein: 4.1 gm

CUCUMBER MOUSSE
SERVES 6
190 mg vitamin C per serving

2 envelopes unflavored gelatin
1 tablespoon lemon juice
½ small onion, thinly sliced
¼ teaspoon salt
Pinch cayenne pepper
½ cup boiling water
½ cup fresh parsley, chopped

2 cups cucumber, peeled, seeded, and diced
¼ teaspoon "C"
1 cup evaporated skim milk
1 cucumber, peeled and thinly sliced (garnish)

Place gelatin, lemon juice, onion slices, salt, cayenne, and boiling water in blender and process on high speed 40 seconds. Remove cover and add parsley, cucumber, and "C." Process 3 more seconds. Refrigerate 30 minutes. Mixture will have begun to set.
Whip evaporated skim milk and fold into cucumbers. Pour cucumber mousse into a lightly oiled 4-cup mold and chill several hours or overnight. When ready to serve, unmold and garnish with cucumber slices.

Per Serving: about ¾-1 cup
Calories: 57
Fat: 0.3 gm
Cholesterol: 2 mg
Sodium: 148 mg
Carbohydrate: 7.4 gm
Protein: 5.9 gm

ORANGE AND ONION SALAD

SERVES 3

102 mg vitamin C per serving • ☆ E

1 large Vidalia onion
2 large oranges, peeled
¼ teaspoon salt (optional)
¼ teaspoon oregano
¼ cup canola or sunflower
  oil
1 tablespoon orange juice

1 tablespoon fresh
  lemon juice
Lettuce
2 tablespoons black olives,
  sliced
¼ teaspoon coarsely
  ground black pepper

Cut onion into 8 thin slices. Cut oranges into 6 slices each. Place onion and oranges in glass dish and marinate 30 minutes in mixture of salt, oregano, oil, and juices. Arrange on lettuce; alternate 3 orange slices and 4 onion slices. Top with remaining marinade and olives. Sprinkle with pepper.

Per Serving: 1½-2 cups
Calories: 253
Fat: 18.7 gm
Cholesterol: 0 mg
Sodium: 299 mg
Carbohydrate: 18.9 gm
Protein: 2.0 gm

ASHMEAD'S COLE SLAW

SERVES 8

265 mg vitamin C per serving

4 cups cabbage, chopped
½ cup carrots, chopped
½ cup celery, chopped
¼ cup green pepper, chopped
¼ cup pickled watermelon
  rind, chopped
¼ cup onions, chopped
  (optional)

¼ cup nonfat sour cream
¼ cup Mayonnaise
  (recipe page 143)
¼ cup vinegar
1 tablespoon celery seed
½ teaspoon "C"

Combine chopped cabbage, carrots, celery, green pepper, rind, and, if desired, onions; set aside. Combine sour cream, Mayonnaise, vinegar, and celery seed, and stir into vegetables, making sure they are all moistened. Let stand in refrigerator at least 3 hours or overnight, if possible. Before serving, add "C."

Per Serving: about ¾ cup
Calories: 84
Fat: 5.9 gm
Cholesterol: 5 mg
Sodium: 77 mg
Carbohydrate: 5.5 gm
Protein: 1.6 gm

SPINACH SALAD
SERVES 6
180 mg vitamin C per serving • ☆ Beta Carotene • ☆ E

1 pound fresh spinach
½ Bermuda onion, thinly
   sliced in rings
6 strips bacon
2 tablespoons corn oil
1 tablespoon lemon juice

¼ teaspoon dry mustard
½ clove garlic, finely minced
   or put through garlic press
½ teaspoon sugar (optional)
¼ teaspoon "C"

Carefully remove spinach leaves from stalks, setting aside any wilted or yellowed leaves—you can add these to your Vegetable Broth (recipe page 27) bag. Thoroughly wash spinach so that you are sure all sand has been washed out. Drain and pat dry with paper towels. When spinach is dry, tear into small pieces and place into salad bowl along with onion rings. Cover with plastic wrap and refrigerate.
Cook bacon until crisp; drain and crumble into small bits. Set aside.
Combine remaining ingredients, except "C" and bacon, in small jar with a tight-fitting lid. Shake until thoroughly mixed. Refrigerate dressing until ready to use. Do not dress salad until ready to serve; otherwise it will become soggy.
Toss spinach and onions with dressing. Add bacon bits and "C," and toss lightly again. Serve in chilled bowls or on plates.

Per Serving: 1¼-1½ cups
Calories: 111
Fat: 7.4 gm
Cholesterol: 5 mg
Sodium: 199 mg
Carbohydrate: 6.2 gm
Protein: 4.8 gm

WATERCRESS AND BEET SALAD

SERVES 6
185 mg vitamin C per serving • ☆ E

2 bunches crisp watercress
2 cups beets, sliced, cooked,
  and chilled

1 recipe Vinaigrette
  Dressing (recipe page 121)

Rinse watercress under cold running water for a moment. Pat dry and separate. Just before serving, combine with sliced beets and toss with Vinaigrette Dressing.

Per Serving: about 1-1¼ cups with dressing
Calories: 151
Fat: 13.8 gm
Cholesterol: 0 mg
Sodium: 225 mg
Carbchydrate: 4.8 gm
Protein: 1.1 gm

WATERCRESS SALAD

SERVES 6
210 mg vitamin C per serving • ☆ E

3 bunches watercress
1 recipe Vinaigrette Dressing
  (recipe page 121)

Rinse watercress under cold running water. Pat dry and separate. Place in plastic bag in refrigerator until ready to serve. Toss with Vinaigrette Dressing just before serving.

Per Serving: about ¾ cup with dressing
Calories: 131
Fat: 13.7 gm
Cholesterol: 0 mg
Sodium: 192 mg
Carbohydrate: 0.7 gm
Protein: 0.5 gm

VINAIGRETTE DRESSING

SERVES 6 (½ CUP)
165 mg vitamin C per serving • ☆ E

2½ tablespoons white wine vinegar
6 tablespoons corn or safflower oil
½ teaspoon salt

¼ teaspoon black pepper, freshly ground
¼ teaspoon dry mustard
¼ teaspoon "C"

Place all ingredients in small jar with a lid. Shake until smooth and thoroughly blended. Serve as accompaniment to chilled artichokes, over cold asparagus, or as salad dressing.
Note: As a variation, you can make this dressing in blender and add 1 green onion and 2 tablespoons of freshly chopped parsley. Blend until smooth.

Per Serving: about 4 teaspoons
Calories: 127
Fat: 13.7 gm
Cholesterol: 0 mg
Sodium: 183 mg
Carbohydrate: 0.1 gm
Protein: trace

BROCCOLI VINAIGRETTE

SERVES 6

111.5 mg vitamin C per serving • ☆ *Beta Carotene* • ☆ *E*

1 bunch fresh broccoli
   (about 1½ lbs.)
1 small onion, sliced
¼ cup fresh lemon or
   lime juice
¼ cup red wine vinegar

2 tablespoons canola or
   sunflower oil
¼ teaspoon hot pepper sauce
2 tablespoons dried tarragon
¼ teaspoon ginger

Wash and trim broccoli; remove leaves and cut into spears. Cook, covered, in 1 inch boiling water 10-15 minutes or until just tender. Drain and place in shallow glass dish; cover with sliced onion. Combine lemon juice, vinegar, oil, hot pepper sauce, tarragon, and ginger in jar or small bowl. Shake or beat to mix well and pour over broccoli and onions. Cover and chill several hours. Drain just before serving.

Per Serving: ½ cup
Calories: 105
Fat: 5.1 gm
Cholesterol: 0 mg
Sodium: 23 mg
Carbohydrate: 9.6 gm
Protein 4.6 gm

HERBED BROCCOLI SALAD

MAKES 6 CUPS

58 mg vitamin C per serving • ☆ *Beta Carotene* • ☆ *E*

2 tablespoons salad oil
2 tablespoons apple-cider
   vinegar
½ teaspoon thyme
½ teaspoon basil leaves,
   crushed

⅛ teaspoon garlic powder
1/16 teaspoon cayenne
1½ cups broccoli medallions*
2 cups carrots, sliced
2½ cups broccoli florets

Combine oil, vinegar, thyme, basil, garlic powder, and cayenne pepper; set aside. In medium saucepan, bring 2 inches water to boil. Add medallions and carrots; simmer 2 minutes. Add broccoli florets; simmer 1 minute.

Drain and place in bowl; toss with dressing. Cover and refrigerate overnight or until chilled. Serve garnished with lettuce leaves, if desired.
*To make medallions, slice broccoli stems crosswise, ¼-inch thick.

Per Serving: about 1 cup
Calories: 91
Fat: 4.9 gm
Cholesterol: 0 mg
Sodium: 51 mg
Carbohydrate: 8.8 gm
Protein: 2.4 gm

BRUSSELS SPROUTS SALAD

SERVES 6-8
157 mg vitamin C per serving

1 pint Brussels sprouts
1 pint cherry tomatoes
6-8 pitted olives

**Vinaigrette Dressing
(recipe page 121)**
1 clove garlic, pressed
Lettuce

Note: Assemble all ingredients for this salad ahead of time, but toss only at last minute.
Remove any wilted leaves from sprouts. Soak sprouts in salted cold water 10 minutes. Drain, wash, and make a cut in the bottom of each bud. Boil 10 minutes in salted water. Sprouts should be just tender, not overcooked. Drain and rinse in cold water. Drain again and cool.
Wash and stem tomatoes. Choose smaller variety. A mixture of red and yellow varieties is very attractive.
Halve olives.
Make Vinaigrette Dressing, adding garlic.
Just before serving, toss sprouts, tomatoes, and olives in dressing.
Serve in salad bowl lined with crisp lettuce leaves.

Per Serving: about ½ cup
Calories: 133
Fat: 11.0 gm
Cholesterol: 0 mg
Sodium: 241 mg
Carbohydrate: 5.2 gm
Protein: 2.3 gm

SUMMER'S HARVEST SALAD

SERVES 8
73 mg vitamin C per serving • ☆ *E*

1 head broccoli, broken
   into small florets
1 cup frozen green peas
1 cup fresh, raw cauliflower,
   broken into small florets
1½ cups celery, chopped
¼ cup green pepper, chopped
¼ cup onion, chopped
½ cup low-fat medium
   cheddar cheese, cut into
   small squares

2 hard-boiled egg whites,
   chopped
1 tablespoon lemon juice
2 tablespoons Mayonnaise
   (recipe page 143)
½ cup of natural sliced
   almonds, toasted

Cook broccoli about 3 minutes or until tender crisp. Drain and cool. Bring peas to boil for 1 minute. Drain and cool. Combine next 6 ingredients. Add lemon juice and toss. Moisten with Mayonnaise. Sprinkle with almonds.

Per Serving: about 1 cup
Calories: 148
Fat: 8.8 gm
Cholesterol: 8 mg
Sodium: 130 mg
Carbohydrate: 9.1 gm
Protein: 7.7 gm

MARINATED ASPARAGUS SALAD

MAKES 5 CUPS
50 mg vitamin C per serving • ☆ *Beta Carotene*

1 (10 oz.) package frozen
   asparagus spears
2 cups cauliflower
   florets
4 medium carrots, cut into
   ⅛" slices
2 hard-boiled egg whites,
   chopped
3 tablespoons apple-cider
   vinegar

2 tablespoons water
⅛ teaspoon cayenne pepper
1 teaspoon instant minced
   onion
½ teaspoon basil leaves
⅛ teaspoon summer savory
⅛ teaspoon celery seed,
   ground
2 teaspoons Dijon mustard

Place asparagus in saucepan with small amount of water. Cover and bring to boil. Lower heat and simmer gently 3 minutes. Cook cauliflower and carrots in small amount of water, simmering for 5 minutes. Drain all vegetables and cool. Cut asparagus into 2-inch pieces, using a diagonal cut. In large bowl, combine asparagus, cauliflower, and carrots. Toss gently. In small bowl, combine remaining ingredients. Mix well. Pour over cooked vegetables. Toss gently. Chill two hours before serving.

Per Serving: 1 cup
Calories: 56
Fat: 0.7 gm
Cholesterol: 0 mg
Sodium: 102 mg
Carbohydrate: 7.5 gm
Protein: 4.4 gm

LEEK SALAD

SERVES 4
255 mg vitamin C per serving • ☆ *E*

3 leeks
1 teaspoon prepared mustard
¼ teaspoon salt
¼ teaspoon black pepper,
freshly ground

1 teaspoon lemon juice
¼ teaspoon "C"
Sugar to taste
¼ cup corn or safflower oil

Trim leeks by cutting off root and most of green top. Cut lengthwise and wash carefully. Leeks are usually filled with sand, so be sure to clean them thoroughly. Pat dry and steam 5-10 minutes or until tender. Cool.
Combine mustard, salt, pepper, lemon juice, "C," sugar, and oil in jar with lid. Shake until well blended. Marinate leeks in dressing at least 1 hour in refrigerator.
Serve salad on chilled plates.

Per Serving: about ¾ cup
Calories: 193
Fat: 14.2 gm
Cholesterol: 0 mg
Sodium: 156 mg
Carbohydrate: 14.7 gm
Protein: 1.7 gm

FRUIT SALAD WITH HONEY MAYONNAISE

SERVES 6
185 mg vitamin C per serving

6 large leaves iceberg lettuce
½ cup fresh strawberries
½ cup fresh blueberries
½ cup sliced fresh peaches
½ cup melon balls, honeydew and cantaloupe combined

½ cup fresh pineapple, cubed
1 recipe Honey Mayonnaise (recipe below)
6 small sprigs fresh mint

To serve salad individually, place a lettuce leaf on each plate. Arrange equal amounts of fresh fruit attractively on plates, leaving room in center for some of Honey Mayonnaise. Garnish dressing with mint, if desired, and serve chilled. Fruit can also be arranged on lettuce leaves on one large platter with Honey Mayonnaise in the center.

Per Serving: about ½ cup
Calories: 388
Fat: 37.5 gm
Cholesterol: 36 mg
Sodium: 110 mg
Carbohydrate: 10.4 gm
Protein: 1.8 gm

HONEY MAYONNAISE

SERVES 6 (1 CUP)
165 mg vitamin C per serving • ☆ E

1 egg
1 tablespoon honey
¼ teaspoon ginger
1 teaspoon dry mustard
1 tablespoon vinegar

¼ teaspoon "C"
¼ teaspoon garlic powder
¼ teaspoon salt
1 cup corn or safflower oil

Combine egg, honey, ginger, mustard, vinegar, "C," garlic powder, salt, and ¼ cup of oil in blender. Process on lowest speed. Immediately begin adding remaining oil in slow, steady stream. Turn off blender when last drop of oil has been added.

Per Serving: about 2½ tablespoons
Calories: 354
Fat: 37.3 gm
Cholesterol: 36 mg
Sodium: 103 mg
Carbohydrate: 3.1 gm
Protein: 1.2 gm

TROPICAL FRESH FRUIT SALAD

SERVES 4
72 mg vitamin C per serving • ☆ E

1 medium-size fresh
  pineapple
1 pint fresh strawberries,
  halved
¼ cup blanched slivered
  almonds, toasted

3 bananas, sliced
2 tablespoons coconut,
  shredded
½ cup plain low-fat yogurt
1 tablespoon packed
  brown sugar

With sharp knife, cut pineapple in half through plume. Remove pineapple from shell; reserve shell. Discard core; cut pineapple into medium-size chunks. In large bowl, combine pineapple, strawberries, almonds, bananas, and coconut; drain excess juices. Combine yogurt and brown sugar; pour over fruit, tossing lightly to mix. Spoon fruit into pineapple shells to serve.

Per Serving: about 1½ cups
Calories: 272
Fat: 6.4 gm
Cholesterol: 3 mg
Sodium: 28 mg
Carbohydrate: 48.0 gm
Protein: 5.2 gm

RAINBOW FRUIT SALAD

SERVES 10
48 mg vitamin C per serving

2 cups (1 large) mango, peeled, sliced
2 cups fresh blueberries
2 bananas, sliced
2 cups strawberries, halved
2 cups green, seedless grapes

2 nectarines, unpeeled, sliced
1 kiwi, peeled, sliced
1 recipe Poppy-Seed Dressing (recipe below)
1 recipe Creamy-Dessert Dressing (recipe page 129)

In glass bowl, arrange layer of mango slices. Continue to layer fresh fruits, using blueberries, bananas, strawberries, grapes, and nectarines. Garnish top with kiwi slices. Serve with Poppy-Seed Dressing as salad or with Creamy-Dessert Dressing as dessert.

Per Serving: about 1¼-1½ cups
Calories: 253
Fat: 11.9 gm
Cholesterol: 1 mg
Sodium: 102 mg
Carbohydrate: 32.4 gm
Protein: 3.4 gm

POPPY-SEED DRESSING

MAKES ¾ CUP
Trace vitamin C per serving

½ cup safflower oil
2 tablespoons white wine vinegar

2 teaspoons onion, grated
2 teaspoons poppy seeds
½ teaspoon dry mustard

Combine all ingredients. Mix well. Serve with Rainbow Fruit Salad (recipe above).

Per Serving: 3½ teaspoons
Calories: 103
Fat: 11.1 gm
Cholesterol: 0 mg
Sodium: trace
Carbohydrate: 0.4 gm
Protein: 0.2 gm

CREAMY-DESSERT DRESSING

MAKES ABOUT 1 CUP
5 mg vitamin C per serving

2 (3 oz.) packages low-fat
cream cheese, at room
temperature
⅓ cup orange juice, freshly
squeezed

2 tablespoons lime juice,
freshly squeezed
1½ tablespoons honey
¼ teaspoon ginger, ground
⅛ teaspoon nutmeg, ground

Combine all ingredients. Mix well. Serve with Rainbow Fruit Salad (recipe
page 128) as a dessert.

Per Serving: about 5 teaspoons
Calories: 29
Fat: 0.1 gm
Cholesterol: 1 mg
Sodium: 97 mg
Carbohydrate: 4.9 gm
Protein: 1.9 gm

ST. PATRICK'S FRUIT PLATTER

SERVES 6
41 mg vitamin C per serving • ☆ E

1 (16 oz.) can Bartlett pear
halves
Leaf lettuce
2 cups iceberg lettuce,
shredded

2-3 kiwi fruit, pared
and sliced
Sweet Poppy-Seed
Dressing (recipe page 130)

Drain pears; reserve 1 tablespoon liquid for Poppy-Seed Dressing. Cut pear
halves in half lengthwise. Line platter with leaf lettuce; arrange shredded
lettuce in center. Place pears and kiwi fruit on lettuce. Drizzle with Poppy-
Seed Dressing.

Per Serving: about 1 cup with dressing
Calories: 162
Fat: 9.5 gm
Cholesterol: 0 mg
Sodium: 9 mg
Carbohydrate: 18.2 gm
Protein: 1.0 gm

SWEET POPPY-SEED DRESSING

MAKES ½ CUP
About 1 mg vitamin C per serving

¼ cup canola oil
2 tablespoon lime juice
1 tablespoon pear liquid

1 teaspoon sugar
⅛ teaspoon dry mustard
1 teaspoon poppy seeds

Combine oil, lime juice, pear liquid, sugar, and mustard. Add poppy seeds; use wire whisk to blend well.

Per Serving: 3-4 teaspoons
Calories: 88
Fat: 9.1 gm
Cholesterol: 0 mg
Sodium: 2 mg
Carbohydrate: 1.3 gm
Protein: trace

SUMMER'S BOUNTY SALAD

SERVES 4
110 mg vitamin C per serving • ☆ E

1 cup bananas, sliced
2 cups orange segments
1 cup almonds, sliced, toasted
1 cup strawberries, sliced
1 cup honeydew melon pieces
2 cups watermelon chunks,
    bite-size

1 cup nectarine slices
1 cup seedless red grapes
1 cup almonds
Dill-Parsley, Lemon-Mint, &
    Chutney-Yogurt dressings
    (recipes pages 131-132)

Chill prepared fruit. Before serving, toss or arrange on plate with almonds. Drizzle with choice of dressings.

Per Serving: 2½ cups without dressing
Calories: 401
Fat: 12.7 gm
Cholesterol: 0 mg
Sodium: 9 mg
Carbohydrate: 47.6 gm
Protein: 9.5 gm

DILL-PARSLEY DRESSING

MAKES 1 CUP
0.5 mg vitamin C per serving

1 cup low-fat yogurt
1 teaspoon dillweed

½ teaspoon lemon juice
1 teaspoon chopped parsley

Combine all ingredients. Mix well and chill.

Per Serving: 2 tablespoons
Calories: 19
Fat: 0.4 gm
Cholesterol: 3 mg
Sodium: 22 mg
Carbohydrate: 2.2 gm
Protein: 1.5 gm

LEMON-MINT DRESSING

MAKES 1 CUP
About 1 mg vitamin C per serving

1 cup low-fat plain yogurt
2 teaspoons lemon juice

1 teaspoon chopped parsley
2 teaspoons mint flakes

Combine all ingredients. Mix well and chill.

Per Serving: 2 tablespoons
Calories: 19
Fat: 0.4 gm
Cholesterol: 3 mg
Sodium: 22 mg
Carbohydrate: 2.2 gm
Protein: 1.5 gm

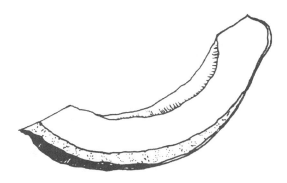

CHUTNEY-YOGURT DRESSING

MAKES 1½ CUPS
About 0.5 mg vitamin C per serving

1 cup low-fat yogurt
4 tablespoons watermelon chutney

4 tablespoons honey

Combine all ingredients. Mix well and chill.

Per Serving: 2 tablespoons
Calories: 18
Fat: 0.1 gm
Cholesterol: 2 mg
Sodium: 8 mg
Carbohydrate: 3.5 gm
Protein: 0.5 gm

ZESTY FRENCH DRESSING

MAKES ABOUT ⅔ CUP
Trace vitamin C per serving • ☆ E

½ cup corn oil
3 tablespoons red wine vinegar
⅛ teaspoon seasoned pepper

⅛ teaspoon basil
1/16 teaspoon hot pepper sauce

Combine all ingredients. Shake together well in covered jar.

Per Serving: about 1 tablespoon
Calories: 83
Fat: 9.1 gm
Cholesterol: 0 mg
Sodium: trace
Carbohydrate: trace
Protein: trace

BLOSSOM SALAD

SERVES 4
83 mg vitamin C per serving • ☆ *E*

1 head iceberg lettuce
1 pint low-fat creamed
   cottage cheese
2 oranges, peeled, sliced
   crosswise, and halved
2 red apples, cored, and sliced
   lengthwise

1 large banana, sliced
¾ cup strawberries, halved
4 small clusters of grapes
   (about 1 cup)
4 mint sprigs
1 recipe Pink Petal Dressing
   (recipe below)

Core, rinse, and thoroughly drain lettuce; refrigerate in plastic bag or plastic crisper. At serving time, remove a few frilly outer lettuce leaves and place on salad plates. Cut remaining lettuce into bite-size chunks and divide equally among lettuce-lined plates. Center ½ cup mound cottage cheese on lettuce. Tuck orange, apple, banana, and strawberry slices into lettuce. Garnish with grapes and mint. Serve with Pink Petal Dressing. Note: Wash grapes and shake off excess water or, dry and coat lightly with beaten egg white; sift powdered sugar over grapes to "frost," if desired.

Per Serving: 1 salad with dressing
Calories: 498
Fat: 22.1 gm
Cholesterol: 31 mg
Sodium: 593 mg
Carbohydrate: 57.2 gm
Protein: 17.3 gm

PINK PETAL DRESSING

MAKES ABOUT 1 CUP
Trace vitamin C per serving

⅔ cup commercial salad dressing
⅔ cup raspberry sherbert

Blend. Serve at once or keep very cold.

Per Serving: ¼-⅓ cup
Calories: 236
Fat: 19.0 gm
Cholesterol: 16 mg
Sodium: 238 mg
Carbohydrate: 15.8 gm
Protein: 0.4 gm

KIWI-FRUIT POTATO VINAIGRETTE

SERVES 6
50 mg vitamin C per serving • ☆ E

1 pound new potatoes,
** cooked and sliced**
⅓ cup thinly sliced celery

3 medium kiwi fruit, pared
** and sliced**
Vinaigrette dressing*

Combine potatoes and celery. Add vinaigrette dressing; gently toss together. Cover and refrigerate several hours. Add kiwi fruit; mix gently.
Vinaigrette dressing: Combine ¼ cup canola or sunflower oil, 3 tablespoons red wine vinegar, 1 tablespoon chopped green onion or chives, ½ teaspoon each sugar and salt, ⅛ teaspoon crushed thyme, and dash bottled hot-pepper sauce. Blend well. Makes about ½ cup.

Per Serving: about ¾ cup
Calories: 157
Fat: 9.3 gm
Cholesterol: 0 mg
Sodium: 195 mg
Carbohydrate: 16.1 gm
Protein: 1.7 gm

RICE-AND-CABBAGE SALAD

SERVES 4
14 mg vitamin C per serving • ☆ E

½ cup brown rice
2 cups boiling water
½ cup seedless raisins
2 cups green cabbage
** (preferably Savoy), shredded**

3 green onions
2 tablespoons mayonnaise

Dressing
2 tablespoons white wine
** vinegar**
½ teaspoon salt
½ teaspoon black pepper

¼ teaspoon Dijon mustard
6 tablespoons salad oil
** (olive, peanut, or corn)**

Pour rice into water. Bring to boil. Cover and simmer 35-40 minutes or until all water is absorbed and rice is just tender. Rinse in cold water. Drain well and cool. Soak raisins in cold water while rice is cooking. Let cabbage stand 30 minutes in very cold water to crisp, then drain or dry in a lettuce spinner. Chop green onions; use green part as well as white. Combine all ingredients for dressing in a jar with a tight-fitting lid. Shake to blend. Set aside. Drain raisins and mix with rice and most of scallions. Season to taste with salt and pepper. Place rice mixture in center of salad bowl. Surround with well-dried cabbage. Just before serving, season cabbage with dressing and garnish with green onions.

Per Serving: about 1¼ cups
Calories: 426
Fat: 26.7 gm
Cholesterol: 6 mg
Sodium: 302 mg
Carbohydrate: 41.5 gm
Protein: 3.7 gm

HAVA-WINNING AVOCADO SALAD

SERVES 6
23 mg vitamin C per serving • ☆ *E*

2 cups cooked chicken, diced
4 cups crisp bean sprouts
2 tablespoons onion, minced
2 tablespoons reduced-sodium soy sauce
⅓ cup Mayonnaise (recipe page 143)

½ teaspoon garlic
3 soft avocados, halved, peeled
Ripe and green olives (for garnish)
1 tomato, cut into wedges

In large bowl, combine all ingredients except avocados, olives, and tomatoes. On plate (lined with lettuce, if desired), fill each avocado half cavity with chicken mixture and garnish with olives and tomato wedges.

Per Serving: ½ avocado + 1 cup filling
Calories: 375
Fat: 29.8 gm
Cholesterol: 53 mg
Sodium: 236 mg
Carbohydrate: 9.0 gm
Protein: 17.2 gm

ENSALADA CON HUEVOS WITH SALSA PIQUANTE

SERVES 6
20 mg vitamin C per serving • ☆ *E*

1 large head iceberg lettuce
½ cup chopped pecans
3 avocados, cut into rings

4 hard-boiled eggs, sliced
1 recipe Salsa Piquante
(recipe below)

Tear lettuce into bite-size pieces and place in salad bowl; sprinkle with pecans. Arrange avocado rings and egg slices on lettuce. Top with Salsa Piquante just before serving.

Per Serving: about 1½ cups
Calories: 466
Fat: 37.6 gm
Cholesterol: 142 mg
Sodium: 64 mg
Carbohydrate: 23.3 gm
Protein: 8.0 gm

SALSA PIQUANTE

MAKES ABOUT 1½ CUPS
10 mg vitamin C per serving • ☆ *E*

⅓ cup corn oil
⅔ cup lemon juice
¼ cup honey
¼ cup vinegar

2 teaspoons paprika
1½ teaspoons dry mustard
½ teaspoon pepper

Combine all ingredients. Blend and chill.

Per Serving: ¼ cup
Calories: 168
Fat: 12.4 gm
Cholesterol: 0 mg
Sodium: 3 mg
Carbohydrate: 13.2 gm
Protein: 0.3 gm

MARINATED FISH SALAD

SERVES 4
27 mg vitamin C per serving • ☆ E

**1 pound fresh cod, halibut,
   red snapper, or a
   combination, cut into
   ½" chunks**
⅓ cup fresh lime juice
**1 cup plum tomatoes,
   seeded and diced**
1 cup yellow pepper, diced

2 green onions, thinly sliced
3 tablespoons olive oil
**2 tablespoons fresh
   coriander, chopped**
**2 teaspoons salt-free lemon
   & herb seasoning**
Endive spears

Lightly rinse fish under cold water and pat dry with paper towels. Place in non-metallic bowl and toss with lime juice. Cover and refrigerate 4 hours, tossing occasionally, until fish is opaque.

Drain off all juices and discard. Add tomatoes, pepper, green onions, oil, coriander, and lemon-and-herb blend to bowl. Toss until well coated. Arrange endive spears on individual plates and top with salad.

Per Serving: 4 oz. marinated fish
Calories: 225
Fat: 11.4 gm
Cholesterol: 42 mg
Sodium: 228 mg
Carbohydrate: 8.6 gm
Protein: 21.0 gm

CAESAR SALAD

SERVES 6
182 mg vitamin C per serving

1 clove garlic, peeled
1 teaspoon dry mustard
2 tablespoons lemon juice
¹⁄₁₆ teaspoon hot pepper sauce
1½ tablespoons olive oil
2 heads romaine lettuce

1 tablespoon low-fat
   Parmesan cheese,
   freshly grated
1 egg, boiled for 60 seconds
¼ teaspoon "C"
½ cup plain croutons

Rub bottom of large wooden salad bowl with garlic clove. Add mustard, lemon juice, and hot pepper sauce. Discard garlic.
Add olive oil and mix quickly and thoroughly.
Wash lettuce, drain, and dry on paper towels. Tear leaves into bite-size pieces and place in salad bowl. Sprinkle with cheese. Break egg and crumble white only into salad, discarding yolk.
Sprinkle croutons over bowl and mix gently with wooden fork and spoon.
Note: Caesar Salad is excellent accompaniment to almost any meal and can also be served as main course for lunch or supper.

Per Serving: about 1-1¼ cups
Calories: 94
Fat: 5.0 gm
Cholesterol: 1 mg
Sodium: 138 mg
Carbohydrate: 8.5 gm
Protein: 3.6 gm

SEAFOOD CAESAR

SERVES 4
19 mg vitamin C per serving • ☆ E

1 head romaine lettuce, torn
   in bite-sized pieces
1 clove garlic, pressed
¼ cup olive oil
¼ teaspoon pepper
¼ teaspoon dry mustard
1½ tablespoons white
   wine vinegar

Juice from ½ lemon
1 package (6-8 oz.) frozen
   Alaskan King crab,
   thawed and drained
1 soft avocado, sliced
½ cup Garlic Croutons
   (recipe page 36)

Place lettuce in large salad bowl. Add pressed garlic to olive oil. Sprinkle garlic oil, pepper, mustard, vinegar, and lemon juice over lettuce. Add crab, avocado, and croutons; toss to lightly coat. Sprinkle Parmesan cheese over salad.

Per Serving: 1-1½ cups
Calories: 405
Fat: 29.9 gm
Cholesterol: 41 mg
Sodium: 289 mg
Carbohydrate: 12.0 gm
Protein: 16.8 gm

WEST INDIES SALAD

SERVES 4
6 mg vitamin C per serving   •   ☆ E

1 Vidalia onion, finely chopped
8 ounces crab meat
4 ounces canola or sunflower oil

4 ounces cider vinegar
4 ounces ice water
¼ teaspoon pepper

It is important to follow each step explicitly. Place half of chopped onion in bowl. Carefully remove any shell from crab meat and add meat to bowl. Add remaining onion. Pour oil over crab meat and onion.Add vinegar and ice water. Toss lightly with pepper; do not stir. Marinate in refrigerator 4-6 hours.

Per Serving: about ¾ cup
Calories: 319
Fat: 27.6 gm
Cholesterol: 24 mg
Sodium: 478 mg
Carbohydrate: 5.3 gm
Protein: 11.1 gm

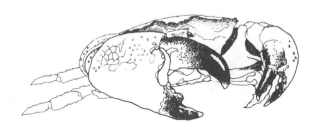

ALMOND CHICKEN SALAD ORIENTAL

SERVES 6

72 mg vitamin C per serving • ☆ *Beta Carotene* • ☆ *E*

1½ cups uncooked rice
2 lemons
¼ cup dark low-sodium
   soy sauce
2 cloves garlic, finely chopped
2 whole chicken breasts,
   skinned, boned, poached
   and cut into cubes
½ pound snow peas or
   green beans, blanched
   and sliced

6 green onions, sliced
½ green pepper, diced
1 large carrot, julienned
   and blanched
⅟₁₆ teaspoon cayenne pepper
1 cup almonds, chopped,
   toasted
Lettuce leaves

Cook rice according to package directions, omitting butter. Meanwhile, grate peel of both lemons; squeeze lemons for juice. Combine lemon peel, juice, soy sauce, and garlic. Marinate chicken in lemon mixture while preparing vegetables. Add hot, cooked rice and vegetables to chicken mixture. Chill. Season with cayenne pepper. Stir in almonds. Serve on lettuce-lined plates.

Per Serving: about 1½ cups
Calories: 290
Fat: 14.0 gm
Cholesterol: 32 mg
Sodium: 686 mg
Carbohydrate: 55.1 gm
Protein: 22.7 gm

SHREDDED-CHICKEN SALAD WITH SESAME SEED DRESSING

SERVES 4

29 mg vitamin C per serving • ☆ Beta Carotene • ☆ E

4 chicken cutlets
1½ teaspoons any salt-free
blended seasoning
1 large cucumber, peeled
and shredded

4 medium carrots, peeled
and shredded
Sesame Seed Dressing
(recipe below)

Bring ½ inch water to boil in large skillet fitted with round wire rack. Sprinkle chicken with blended seasoning. Place chicken on rack, cover pan, and steam 8 minutes, until springy to touch. Remove and let cool. Tear into long shreds. To serve, divide cucumber and carrot among 4 plates. Top with chicken and dressing.

Per Serving: 1 cup with dressing
Calories: 270
Fat: 13.1 gm
Cholesterol: 63 mg
Sodium: 151 mg
Carbohydrate: 14.5 gm
Protein: 22.6 gm

SESAME SEED DRESSING

SERVES 4

13 mg vitamin C per serving • ☆ E

½ cup orange juice
2 tablespoons safflower oil
2 tablespoons red wine vinegar
2 teaspoons sesame seeds,
toasted

1 teaspoon salt-free extra
spicy seasoning
1 teaspoon low-sodium
soy sauce

In small bowl, combine all ingredients. Pour over chicken and toss.

Per Serving: about 3 tablespoons
Calories: 91
Fat: 7.7 gm
Cholesterol: 0 mg
Sodium: 58 mg
Carbohydrate: 3.9 gm
Protein: 0.8 gm

JAPANESE CHICKEN SALAD
SERVES 4-6
82 mg vitamin C per serving • ☆ E

Dressing

½ cup corn oil

3 tablespoons Oriental
sesame oil

3 tablespoons vinegar

2 teaspoons low-sodium soy
sauce

1 teaspoon ginger, grated

Salad

1 package (3 oz.) soup noodles,
uncooked

7 cups green cabbage,
thinly sliced

2 cups red cabbage,
thinly sliced

2 tablespoons green onion,
thinly sliced

2 cups chicken, cooked
and shredded

1 cup slivered almonds,
toasted

2 cups pea pods, blanched

Combine dressing ingredients and mix well. Marinate noodles in dressing until tender (about 1 hour). Combine remaining salad ingredients, except pea pods, in large bowl. Once noodles are tender, pour noodles and dressing over salad; toss to combine. To serve, arrange pea pods on large serving plate and spoon salad into center.

Per Serving: 2¼-2½ cups
Calories: 510
Fat: 35.5 gm
Cholesterol: 56 mg
Sodium: 119 mg
Carbohydrate: 24.6 gm
Protein: 23 gm

MAYONNAISE

SERVES 6 (1¼ CUPS)

50 mg vitamin C per serving • ☆ E

1 egg
½ teaspoon dry mustard
1 tablespoon white wine vinegar

¼ teaspoon "C"
1 cup corn or safflower
oil

Break egg into blender. Add mustard, salt, vinegar, and "C." Add ¼ cup of oil and cover. Process on low. Once processing has begun pour in remaining oil in thin steady stream. Mix only until last bit of oil is added.
Note: Homemade mayonnaise is delicious and easy to make using this method. It can also be flavored with an endless number of herbs and seasonings (dill, tarragon, parsley, curry) as well as green pepper, watercress, spinach, anchovy, chives, and anything else you think sounds good.

Per Serving: about 3 tablespoons
Calories: 342
Fat: 37.2 gm
Cholesterol: 36 mg
Sodium: 11 mg
Carbohydrate: 0.3 gm
Protein: 1.2 gm

GREEN MAYONNAISE

SERVES 6 (1¼ CUPS)

168 mg vitamin C per serving • ☆ E

1 cup Mayonnaise (recipe above)
4 tablespoons minced fresh green herbs
(such as parsley, chives, tarragon, basil)

Stir minced fresh herbs into Mayonnaise and serve, chilled, with fish.

Per Serving: about 3 tablespoons
Calories: 343
Fat: 37.2 gm
Cholesterol: 36 mg
Sodium: 12 mg
Carbohydrate: 0.5 gm
Protein: 1.4 gm

ROUQUEFORT DRESSING
SERVES 8 (2 CUPS)
250 mg vitamin C per serving

8 ounces nonfat cream cheese, cubed
4 ounces blue or Roquefort cheese
½ cup skim milk

1 tablespoon lemon juice
½ clove garlic
½ teaspoon tarragon
¼ teaspoon pepper
½ teaspoon "C"

Combine all ingredients in blender for 30 seconds or until smooth. Scrape down sides with rubber spatula as needed.

Per Serving: about ¼ cup
Calories: 94
Fat: 4.5 gm
Cholesterol: 14 mg
Sodium: 425 mg
Carbohydrate: 6.5 gm
Protein: 6.6 gm

SAVORY CARROT DRESSING
SERVES 10 (1¼ CUPS)
3 mg vitamin C per serving • ☆ *Beta Carotene* • ☆ *E*

1 tablespoon cornstarch
¾ cup canned carrot juice, divided
¼ cup green onion, chopped
3 tablespoons cider vinegar

2 tablespoons canola or sunflower oil
½ teaspoon garlic, crushed
½ teaspoon salt (optional)
⅛ teaspoon ground black pepper

In small saucepan, blend cornstarch with ¼ cup of carrot juice. Stir in remaining carrot juice. Stir over medium heat until mixture boils and thickens, about 1 minute. Remove from heat. Stir in green onions, vinegar, oil, garlic, salt, and black pepper. Cool. Serve over mixed greens, if desired.

Per Serving: 2 tablespoons
Calories: 38
Fat: 2.8 grams
Cholesterol: 0 mg
Sodium: 116 mg
Carbohydrates: 2.7 gm
Protein: 0.2 gm

HERBED CARROT SALAD DRESSING

MAKES 1 CUP
4 mg vitamin C per serving • ☆ Beta Carotene • ☆ E

½ cup carrot juice
¼ cup canola or sunflower oil
3 tablespoons lemon juice
2 tablespoons nonfat
  dry milk
1 teaspoon onion powder
½ teaspoon dry powdered
  mustard

½ teaspoon thyme leaves,
  crushed
½ teaspoon grated lemon
  peel
½ teaspoon salt
⅛ teaspoon ground black
  pepper

In jar with tight-fitting lid, combine carrot juice, oil, lemon juice, dry milk, onion and mustard powders, thyme, lemon peel, salt, and pepper. Shake until blended. Let stand 1 hour. Serve over salad greens, if desired.

Per Serving: 2 tablespoons
Calories: 81
Fat: 7.1 grams
Cholesterol: trace
Sodium: 153 mg
Carbohydrates: 3.3 gm
Protein: 0.9 gm

Desserts

So many fruits, packed with natural "C," make wonderful desserts, especially when served in a decorative bowl and served with coffee. If you enjoy your fresh fruits peeled and sliced, sprinkling them with vitamin C is the ideal way to keep them from darkening. Apples, apricots, peaches, pears, bananas, avocados, and persimmons all discolor from exposure to air. As you prepare your fruit, coat sliced pieces with a mixture of one teaspoon of crystalline ascorbic acid to one cup water. For good measure, sprinkle a dash of "C" over the top of the fruit, along with sugar or shredded coconut, if desired. Your fruit dessert will look as good as it tastes.

Ideally, dessert is intended to refresh the mouth and taste buds after the solid fare of the meal's main course. Desserts offer sweet and sometimes sour contrasts to the enveloping flavors of entrée courses that went before. The word *dessert* is French in origin, deriving from *desservir,* meaning "to clear away dishes from a table."

GRAPES IN SOUR CREAM

SERVES 6

170 mg vitamin C per serving • ☆ E

6 cups seedless grapes
½ cup sour cream
3 tablespoons brown sugar

½ teaspoon ground ginger
¼ teaspoon "C"

Place grapes in chilled serving bowl. Combine all other ingredients except "C" and add to bowl. Mix gently so that grapes are coated.
Chill. Add "C" and stir again just before serving.

Per Serving: about 1 cup
Calories: 189
Fat: 4.5 gm
Cholesterol: 9 mg
Sodium: 19 mg
Carbohydrate: 35.3 gm
Protein: 1.6 gm

LEMON PUFFS

MAKES 30

60 mg vitamin C per serving

1½ cups sugar
2 tablespoons light corn syrup
¼ cup water
1 egg white, stiffly beaten

¼ teaspoon lemon juice
Yellow food coloring
¼ teaspoon "C"

Combine sugar, syrup, and water; stir until sugar dissolves. Cook to soft-ball stage (234° F). Slowly pour over egg white, beating until mixture holds shape when dropped from spoon. Add drop or two of lemon juice.
Color delicate yellow. Add "C." Swirl from teaspoon onto waxed paper.

Per Serving: 2 puffs
Calories: 89
Fat: 0 gm
Cholesterol: 0 mg
Sodium: 7 mg
Carbohydrate: 22.0 gm
Protein: 0.2 gm

FROZEN LEMON SOUFFLÉ

SERVES 8
260 mg vitamin C per serving

6 egg yolks
1¾ cups sugar, plus 2 teaspoons
¾ cup fresh lemon juice
1 lemon rind, grated

¾ cup evaporated skim milk
¼ teaspoon "C"
6 egg whites

In heavy saucepan, beat egg yolks and 1½ cups sugar with electric mixer. Beat a few minutes until yolks become lighter in color. Add lemon juice and blend. Beat constantly for 10 minutes over very low heat or until mixture thickens like custard.
Scrape into another bowl and stir in grated lemon rind. Chill thoroughly.
Prepare a 5-cup soufflé dish. Fasten a collar of waxed paper around dish so that it rises about 2 inches above rim. Overlap paper and secure it with paper clips.
Whip ½ cup skim milk with electric mixer. When it begins to thicken, add 2 teaspoons sugar. Continue beating until stiff.
Remove egg mixture from refrigerator and fold in "C." Then fold in whipped cream.
In another bowl, beat egg whites. When they begin to mound, sprinkle in ¼ cup sugar and continue until stiff peaks are formed.
Gently fold whites into soufflé mixture. Do not overmix. Gently pour mixture into prepared soufflé dish and place in freezer for several hours or overnight.
Just before serving remove collar. Whip remaining ¼ cup skim milk and use for decoration.

Per Serving: about 1 cup
Calories: 263
Fat: 3.9 gm
Cholesterol: 161 mg
Sodium: 90 mg
Carbohydrate: 50.1 gm
Protein: 6.7 gm

SPARKLING FRUITS WITH LEMON SAUCE

SERVES 6

30 mg vitamin C per serving   •   ☆ Beta Carotene

4 teaspoons honey
1 tablespoon cornstarch
1 cup water
1 teaspoon lemon rind, grated
¼ cup fresh lemon juice
**2 peaches (2 cups), peeled,
   sliced**

2 plums (2 cups), sliced
**1 cup fresh or frozen
   blueberries**
**1 cup fresh strawberries,
   sliced**

In small saucepan, whisk cornstarch and water. Add honey, lemon rind, and lemon juice. Cook over medium heat, stirring constantly until mixture thickens and boils. Cook 2 minutes. Cool. Prepare fruit. Place in large bowl and add lemon sauce. Cover. Refrigerate 1½-2 hours. Serve plain or over yogurt.

Per Serving: 1 cup
Calories: 96
Fat: 0.5 gm
Cholesterol: 0 mg
Sodium: 4 mg
Carbohydrate: 22.8 gm
Protein: 1.1 gm

LEMON SHERBET

SERVES 6

175 mg vitamin C per serving

2 cups water
¾ cup sugar, plus 2 tablespoons
1 teaspoon grated lemon rind
**2 teaspoons unflavored gelatin
   soaked in 4 tablespoons
   cold water**

⅛ teaspoon salt
⅓ cup lemon juice
¼ teaspoon "C"

Combine water, ¾ cup sugar, and lemon rind in saucepan. Bring to boil, reduce heat, and simmer for 10 minutes. Remove from heat and stir in gelatin and water mixture. Add salt and strain through a very fine sieve. Chill. When thoroughly chilled, stir in lemon juice, "C," and remaining 2 tablespoons sugar. Return to freezer until ready to serve. Stir every hour during freezing to keep sherbet smooth.

Per Serving: about ½ cup
Calories: 124
Fat: trace
Cholesterol: 0 mg
Sodium: 47 mg
Carbohydrate: 30.3 gm
Protein: 0.4 gm

ORANGE RUM SHERBET

SERVES 6
190 mg vitamin C per serving

2 teaspoons unflavored gelatin
¾ cup cold water
¾ cup sugar
1 cup orange juice
1 tablespoon lime juice

½ cup light rum
1 tablespoon grated orange
rind
¹⁄₁₆ teaspoon salt
¼ teaspoon "C"

Soften gelatin in ¼ cup of water.
In saucepan, combine remaining ½ cup water and sugar. Boil for 1 minute. Add gelatin and stir until dissolved. Add orange and lime juices, rum, orange rind, and salt. Strain and cool. Stir in "C."
Pour cooled mixture into freezing tray. Freeze until sherbet becomes slushy—a couple of hours. Remove from freezer and beat with electric mixer until smooth. Return to freezing tray and freeze. Stir sherbet several times during freezing until it is almost firm. The sherbet should be a bit slushy when served.

Per Serving: about ½ cup
Calories: 142
Fat: 0.1 gm
Cholesterol: 0 mg
Sodium: 25 mg
Carbohydrate: 31.3 gm
Protein: 0.6 gm

FRESH RASPBERRY SAUCE FOR ICE CREAM

SERVES 6

35 mg vitamin C per tablespoon

2 cups fresh raspberries
½ cup sugar (more if berries are especially tart) or honey
1 tablespoon cornstarch
¾ tablespoon lemon juice

¼ teaspoon "C"
1 tablespoon cognac (optional)

Mash raspberries with sugar. Heat in saucepan, stirring frequently and bringing to boil. Strain and add extra sugar if necessary. Cool.

Mix cornstarch with 2 tablespoons of raspberry juice. Heat remaining juice to boiling; add cornstarch. Cook, stirring constantly until sauce is thickened. Cool. Add lemon juice, "C," and cognac.

Serve over vanilla ice cream.

Per Serving: about 1 cup
Calories: 102 per 2-3 tablespoons
Fat: 0.2 gm
Cholesterol: 0 mg
Sodium: 2 mg
Carbohydrate: 23.4 gm
Protein: 0.4 gm

LIME PIE

SERVES 6

180 mg vitamin C per serving

1½ cups granulated sugar
1 envelope unflavored gelatin
3 egg yolks
¾ cup evaporated skim milk
¾ cup fresh lime juice, strained
3 tablespoons grated lime rind
½ teaspoon "C"

3 egg whites
1 (9") pastry shell, baked
1 cup evaporated skim milk, icy cold
2 tablespoons confectioners' sugar

Mix granulated sugar and gelatin in saucepan. Beat egg yolks into sugar mixture. Slowly stir in ¾ cup evaporated milk. Cook mixture over medium heat, stirring constantly, until it begins to coat spoon. Do not let mixture boil.

Pour mixture into large bowl and beat in lime juice and 2 tablespoons lime rind. Cool to room temperature.

When custard is cool, stir in "C." Beat egg whites until they form stiff peaks. With rubber spatula stir in ¼ of egg whites. Pour custard over remaining egg whites and gently fold together. Do not overmix.

Pour filling into prepared pastry shell and refrigerate for at least 2 hours. Just before serving, whip 1 cup chilled evaporated skim milk with 2 tablespoons confectioners' sugar. Spread over top of pie and garnish with remaining tablespoon of lime rind.

Per Serving: ⅙ pie
Calories: 437
Fat: 10.8 gm
Cholesterol: 110 mg
Sodium: 274 mg
Carbohydrate: 72.9 gm
Protein: 11.8 gm

LIME DIVINITY

MAKES 30 PIECES
16 mg vitamin C per piece

1½ cups sugar	1 egg white, stiffly beaten
½ cup light corn syrup	⅛ teaspoon "C"
¼ cup hot water	½ teaspoon lime juice
Few drops food coloring	½ cup nuts, coarsely chopped
½ teaspoon vanilla	

Combine sugar, corn syrup, water, food coloring, and vanilla. Cover and place over moderate heat. Heat to boiling. Remove cover after five minutes. Cook to very hard-ball stage (260° F). Remove from heat, cooling slightly, and gradually add to stiffly beaten egg white, beating constantly until very stiff. Let cool, stirring occasionally. Stir in vitamin C, lime juice, and nut meats.

Drop from buttered teaspoon onto buttered cookie sheet.

Per Serving: 2 pieces
Calories: 142
Fat: 2.5 gm
Cholesterol: 0 mg
Sodium: 21 mg
Carbohydrate: 28.8 gm
Protein: 0.8 gm

BLACKBERRY BREAD RING

MAKES 1 RING, ABOUT 10 SLICES
6 mg vitamin C per serving • ☆ E

1½ cups whole-wheat flour
½ teaspoon salt
½ teaspoon soda
2 teaspoons cinnamon
¾ cup packed brown sugar
½ cup corn oil
2 eggs

1 teaspoon vanilla
½ cup chopped nuts
1 cup crushed blackberries
(fresh or frozen)
2 tablespoons graham-
cracker crumbs

Combine first 5 ingredients. Stir in oil, eggs, and vanilla just until dry ingredients are moistened. Fold in nuts and berries. Lightly coat 6-cup
microwaveable ring mold with vegetable spray. Sprinkle with graham-
cracker crumbs. Spoon batter into ring mold; cover with wax paper. Microwave on Medium (50%) 10 minutes; rotate ring mold once. Microwave on
High (100%) until no longer doughy (2-3 minutes).
Conventional preparation: Bake in preheated 350° F oven until tender, 45-50
minutes.

Per Serving: 1 slice
Calories: 260
Fat: 10.7 gm
Cholesterol: 43 mg
Sodium: 180 mg
Carbohydrate: 35.5 gm
Protein: 4.9 gm

STRAWBERRY BAVARIAN CREAM

SERVES 6
190 mg vitamin C per serving

1 package (10 oz.) frozen
strawberries
2 envelopes unflavored gelatin
¼ cup cold skim milk
¼ cup sugar

½ cup egg substitute
1 heaping cup crushed ice
1 cup evaporated skim milk
¼ teaspoon "C"

Thaw strawberries; drain, reserving juice. Heat ½ cup juice from strawberries to simmering. Combine gelatin, juice, and milk in an electric blender. Cover and process on medium speed 40 seconds.

Add sugar and egg substitute. Cover and process 5 seconds. Add drained berries and process 5 more seconds. Add ice and evaporated skim milk. Cover and process 20 seconds. Stir in "C."

Pour Strawberry Bavarian Cream into a lightly oiled 4-cup mold. Chill for several hours. Unmold just before serving.

Per Serving: ¾ -1 cup
Calories: 122
Fat: 0.1 gm
Cholesterol: 2 mg
Sodium: 85 mg
Carbohydrate: 22.4 gm
Protein: 7.6 gm

STRAWBERRIES ROMANOFF
SERVES 6
325 mg vitamin C per serving

2 pints fresh strawberries
½ cup confectioners' sugar
2 tablespoons Cointreau

1 tablespoon cognac
1 cup evaporated skim milk
¼ teaspoon "C"

Wash, hull, drain, and dry strawberries. Sprinkle sugar over berries in mixing bowl. Pour in Cointreau and cognac. Refrigerate 2 hours, until thoroughly chilled.

Just before serving, whip evaporated skim milk until stiff. Fold in "C" and strawberries. Serve at once.

Per Serving: about 1 cup
Calories: 127
Fat: 0.5 gm
Cholesterol: 2 mg
Sodium: 51 mg
Carbohydrate: 24.1 gm
Protein: 3.9 gm

FROZEN STRAWBERRY PIE

SERVES 8

36 mg vitamin C per serving • ☆ E

2 cups strawberries, puréed
1 (8 oz.) package sugar-free
vanilla pudding-and-pie-
filling mix

2 cups low-fat plain yogurt
2 tablespoons corn oil
margarine
2 cups granola

Combine strawberries and pudding mix in 1-quart microwaveable container. Microwave on High until mixture thickens and boils, 5-6 minutes; stir 2-3 times. Stir in yogurt.

In 9-inch pie plate, microwave margarine on High until melted, 30 seconds-1 minute. Crush granola very fine, using food processor or blender. Stir into melted margarine and press crumbs over bottom and sides of pie plate. Microwave on High until lightly toasted, 1-2 minutes. Pour strawberry mixture into pie shell and freeze until firm, about 4 hours. Let pie sit at room temperature about 30 minutes before serving. Garnish each serving with fresh strawberries.

Conventional preparation: Cook strawberries and pudding mix in medium saucepan over low heat. Bring to boil 1 minute to thicken; stir constantly. Melt margarine in small saucepan and add granola crumbs. Press into pie plate and bake in preheated 350° F oven 5-10 minutes. Continue as directed in microwave recipe.

Per Serving: ⅛ pie
Calories: 226
Fat: 7.8 gm
Cholesterol: 3 mg
Sodium: 294 mg
Carbohydrate: 33.2 gm
Protein: 5.5 gm

BREAKFAST FRUIT PIZZA

SERVES 8
62 mg vitamin C per serving • ☆ E

1¼ cups all-purpose flour
¾ cup natural bran flakes, crushed
1 teaspoon baking powder
2 tablespoons honey, divided
⅔ cup skim milk
¼ cup canola or sunflower oil
1 (15 oz.) container part-skim milk ricotta cheese

1 teaspoon vanilla extract
2 cups sliced strawberries
2 medium oranges, peeled and sliced
2 kiwi fruit, pared and sliced
½ cup apricot jam, if desired

Preheat oven to 425° F.

Combine flour, cereal, 1 tablespoon honey, and baking powder. Add milk and oil. Stir with fork until mixture forms ball. With greased fingers, press dough into 14-inch round pizza pan or 15 x 10-inch jelly roll pan sprayed with nonstick spray or greased lightly. Shape edge to form rim. Bake 20 minutes or until golden brown. Cool. Combine ricotta, remaining 1 tablespoon honey, and vanilla. Spread over crust. Arrange fruit over cheese mixture in any desired pattern. Heat apricot jam over low heat, stirring constantly until softened. Spoon over fruit to glaze.

Per Serving: ⅛ pie
Calories: 337
Fat: 9.2 gm
Cholesterol: 8 mg
Sodium: 163 mg
Carbohydrate: 51.5 gm
Protein: 10.4 gm

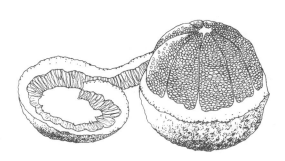

Beverages

With beverages, we hit the high "C" of the whole vitamin song. Here is the shelf whereon your treasure lies, easily at hand. Fresh juices brisk in the morning sun; and later in the day, cool in the setting sun for an evening's relaxation and refreshment. So that you will know where the "C" treasures lie in juices, we've included them in the vitamin C chart on page 176.

Quite obviously, drinking orange juice every morning is going to be helpful. But we should examine other opportunities in cool drinks and even socially acceptable cocktails that provide the "C" along with the zip. Especially rich in beta carotene, carrot juice is also a delightful and healthful breakfast drink.

ICED TEA

SERVES 4

250 mg vitamin C per serving

Slightly more than 1 quart cold tap water (or distilled water)
3 tea bags
¼ cup sugar

¼ teaspoon "C"
1 tablespoon lemon juice, freshly squeezed
4 sprigs fresh mint

Be sure to use cold tap water or cold distilled water when making iced tea.
If water is warm or hot, tea will be cloudy.
Bring cold water to boil and turn off heat. Add tea bags and let sit until water turns a medium to dark brown tea color. Remove bags and cool.
Add sugar, "C," and lemon juice when tea is cool; refrigerate.
Serve over ice with a sprig of fresh mint.

Per Serving: 8 oz.
Calories: 53
Fat: 0 gm
Cholesterol: 0 mg
Sodium: 1 mg
Carbohydrate: 12.9 gm
Protein: trace

STRAWBERRY SHAKE

SERVES 4

300 mg vitamin C per serving

1 cup fresh strawberries
1 cup orange juice, freshly squeezed

3 tablespoons sugar
1 cup ice
¼ teaspoon "C"

Combine all ingredients in blender; process until liquefied. Serve ice cold.

Per Serving: about 6 oz.
Calories: 78
Fat: 0.3 gm
Cholesterol: 0 mg
Sodium: 2 mg
Carbohydrate: 18.0 gm
Protein: 0.7 gm

APPLE SWIZZLE

SERVES 4
250 mg vitamin C per serving

¼ teaspoon Angostura bitters
¾ cup apple brandy
½ cup rum

¼ cup lime juice
4 teaspoons sugar
¼ teaspoon "C"

Pour ingredients into glass pitcher with plenty of crushed ice. Stir vigorously until glass frosts. Strain into glasses and serve.

Per Serving: about 3 oz.
Calories: 195
Fat: trace
Cholesterol: 0 mg
Sodium: trace
Carbohydrate: 14.8 gm
Protein: 0.1 gm

ORANGE-PINEAPPLE PUNCH

SERVES 8
180 mg vitamin C per serving

3 cups orange juice
3 cups pineapple juice
¼ cup lemon juice

1 pint soda water
¼ teaspoon "C"

Combine all ingredients in large pitcher. Add ice cubes. Chill until ready to serve.
Note: Gin or vodka may be added if desired.

Per Serving: about 8 oz.
Calories: 101
Fat: 0.3 gm
Cholesterol: 0 mg
Sodium: 2 mg
Carbohydrate: 23.3 gm
Protein: 1.0 gm

ORANGE-APRICOT NECTAR

SERVES 1
36 mg vitamin C per serving

1 scoop ice
2 apricot halves
2 ounces orange juice

3 teaspoons lemon juice
3 teaspoons simple syrup

In blender, combine 1 scoop crushed ice, apricot halves, fresh-squeezed orange juice, fresh-squeezed lemon juice, and syrup. Serve in champagne glass and garnish with ½ orange slice.

Per Serving: 8 oz.
Calories: 108
Fat: 0.2 gm
Cholesterol: 0 mg
Sodium: 3 mg
Carbohydrate: 25.0 gm
Protein: 1.0 gm

TROPICAL CRANAPPLE PUNCH

MAKES ABOUT 2 QUARTS
69 mg vitamin C per serving

1½ quarts cranberry juice
2 cups apple juice
1 tablespoon sugar
10 whole cloves
2 (2") cinnamon sticks

Ice cubes
1 (12 oz.) bottle club soda
Strawberries
Melon balls

In large saucepan, combine cranberry juice, apple juice, sugar, cloves, and cinnamon; bring to boil. Reduce heat and simmer, uncovered, 10 minutes. Strain and discard spices; chill. Just before serving, pour juice over ice cubes in punch bowl or large pitcher. Stir in club soda. Serve in punch cups, and garnish with skewers of strawberries and melon balls, if desired.

Per Serving: 8 oz.
Calories: 127
Fat: 0.1 gm
Cholesterol: 0 mg
Sodium: 19 mg
Carbohydrate: 31.4 gm
Protein: trace

COCONUT CREEPER

SERVES 1
29 mg vitamin C per serving • ☆ E

1 scoop ice
2 oz. orange juice
1 oz. pineapple juice
1 oz. coconut cream

1 oz. light cream
Pineapple wedge
Cherry

In a blender, finely crush ice. Pour into glass and add 2 ounces fresh-squeezed orange juice, 1 ounce pineapple juice, 1 ounce coconut cream, and 1 ounce cream. Garnish with pineapple and cherry.

Per Serving: 8 oz.
Calories: 190
Fat: 12.7 gm
Cholesterol: 2 mg
Sodium: 33 mg
Carbohydrate: 16.1 gm
Protein: 2.3 gm

MINT 'N SPICE FRUITADE

MAKES 3 QUARTS
54 mg vitamin C per serving

4 teaspoons crushed mint
flakes
2 whole nutmegs, cracked
2½ quarts water
1 tablespoon sugar

1 (12 oz.) can frozen orange-juice concentrate, thawed
1 (6 oz.) can frozen sugarless lemonade concentrate, thawed

Tie mint flakes and nutmegs in cheesecloth. In large saucepan, combine water, sugar, and bag of spices; bring to boil. Reduce heat and simmer, covered, 15 minutes. Remove and discard spice bag. Pour spiced water into large pitcher; stir in orange juice and lemonade; chill. Serve with ice cubes. Garnish with orange slices, if desired.

Per Serving: 8 oz.
Calories: 88
Fat: 0.1 gm
Cholesterol: 0 mg
Sodium: 2 mg
Carbohydrate: 20.5 gm
Protein: 0.9 gm

HONEY-LEMON BERRY DRINK
SERVES 6
23 mg vitamin C per serving

2 (8 oz. each) containers low-fat lemon yogurt
3 tablespoons honey

20 (about 1½ cups) whole frozen unsweetened strawberries

Combine all ingredients in blender; cover. Process on high speed until almost smooth. Serve immediately in tall, chilled glasses.

Per Serving: about 5 oz.
Calories: 118
Fat: 1.4 gm
Cholesterol: 7 mg
Sodium: 55 mg
Carbohydrate: 22.4 gm
Protein: 3.8 gm

SPICED ICE CUBES
Add vitamin C to your drinks by using one of these variations.

MAKES 1 TRAY
8 mg vitamin C per serving

Combine 2 cups orange juice with ¾ teaspoon whole cloves (for grapefruit juice, iced tea).

Per Serving: 1 cube
Calories: 11
Fat: 0.1 gm
Cholesterol: 0 mg
Sodium: 1 mg
Carbohydrate: 2.2 gm
Protein: 0.2 gm

MAKES 1 TRAY
2.5 mg vitamin C per serving

Combine 2 cups pineapple juice with 2 teaspoons ground ginger (for club soda, iced tea, orange juice).

Per Serving: 1 cube
Calories: 13
Fat: Trace
Cholesterol: 0 mg
Sodium: 1 mg
Carbohydrate: 3.0 gm
Protein: 0.1 gm

SPICED ICE CUBES *(continued)*

MAKES 1 TRAY
1.5 mg vitamin C per serving

2 cups lemonade with 1 teaspoon whole allspice (for iced tea, cola, club soda).

Per Serving: 1 cube
Calories: 9
Fat: Trace
Cholesterol: 0 mg
Sodium: trace
Carbohydrate: 2.1 gm
Protein: trace

MAKES 1 TRAY
4 mg vitamin C per serving

2 cups tomato juice (low sodium, optional) with 4½ teaspoons Italian seasoning (for tomato juice, mixed vegetable juice, clam and tomato cocktail).

Per Serving: 1 cube
Calories: 5
Fat: Trace
Cholesterol: 0 mg
Sodium: 74 mg
Carbohydrate: 0.9 gm
Protein: 0.2 gm

Tie whole spices or flakes in cheesecloth (not necessary with ground spices). In small saucepan, combine liquid with spice. Bring to boil. Reduce heat and simmer, covered, for 15 minutes. Remove cheesecloth. Let cool to room temperature. Pour into one ice-cube tray with divider. Freeze until solid.

Serving suggestions: To put frosting on glass, so to speak, give your glassware the "cold shoulder" by placing wet glasses in freezer or by burying them in shaved ice until they are frosty white.

Don't forget to add a twist of citrus peel. Not only does it add character, it gives a delightful fresh aroma to a drink.

Here's an easy way to remove the peel: Using a sharp pointed knife, cut off a thin slice of lemon from each end. Set lemon on cutting board, either end down. Cut peel in strips from top to bottom using tip of knife. Use peeled fruit to make fresh juice.

For great garnishes, try a lemon peel twist, skewered with a cherry. Hollow out a grapefruit or an orange shell and freeze it. You'll have more than a glass for class. You can also just freeze citrus on a stick for a catchy citrus swizzler.

Home Freezing
of Fruits

Vitamin C's finest hour in the kitchen comes at fruit-freezing time. It is always a happy discovery when a beginning cook first uses "C" to prevent darkening during preparation of apples, peaches, and other fruits that brown quickly when peeled.

Grandmother tried to keep fruit from darkening with citric acid or lemon juice. Alas, too much made the fruit sour or masked its flavor. Ascorbic acid not only prevents darkening, but it also preserves flavor and adds nutrition as well. It does a dramatic job right before your eyes; the peeled apples and peaches dropped into ascorbic acid solution just won't darken.

You will find on the market several different antidarkening preparations made of ascorbic acid combined with sugar. Ascorbic acid is the only active ingredient in these mixtures, but because of its dilution with other materials, this form is far more expensive than pure ascorbic acid. For reasons of economy, we suggest using "C" in crystalline or powder form. If pure vitamin C is not available and you must use commercial ascorbic acid mixtures to which sugar has been added, follow the manufacturer's instructions. Volume for volume, a teaspoon of the mixture will not be as effective as a teaspoon of pure "C."

For a few fruits, citric acid or lemon juice will keep the fruit from darkening, but it is not as effective as ascorbic acid.

Frozen carefully, the natural vitamin C in fruit remains remarkably stable. Obtain your fruit at the height of the season when it is fully ripe. Simply buy or pick extra with your freezing plan in mind. If you have any doubts as to how well a fruit will freeze, test a small amount before freezing large quantities.

You can have June in January by home freezing your fruits. There is no "out of season" for products of your orchard or garden when you have a home freezer.

Preparation for Freezing

Prepare fruit much as you would for serving. Peel fruit, leave whole or slice, crush, or purée. Large fruits will usually have a more attractive texture if they are cut into pieces or crushed before freezing. If individual fruits are less than perfect, it is usually best to pack them crushed or puréed.

All fruits will need careful washing in cold water. Handle a small quantity at a time, gently, to avoid bruising. Do not allow the fruit to stand in water, as soaking will impair the texture and cause loss of food value and flavor, as well as any natural "C." A colander or wire basket may be used to lift the fruit out of the water and to allow it to drain thoroughly.

For crushing soft fruits, use a wire potato masher, a wire pastry blender, or a slotted spoon. Firm-textured fruits may be put through a food chopper. To purée fruit, use a colander, food press, or strainer.

Do not use galvanized ware in contact with fruit or fruit juices, as the acid in fruit can dissolve zinc, which is poisonous, from the galvanized surface. Contact with iron, chipped enamelware, or poor-quality tinware may give the fruit a metallic off-flavor.

For best results, use containers and utensils made of glass, plastic, aluminum, or stainless steel.

Methods of Packing

The method of packing will depend on the type of fruit and how it is to be used.

Syrup pack is preferred when the fruit is to be served as an uncooked dessert. The fruit is washed and prepared, then placed in containers and covered with syrup to which "C" has been added. Allow head space; seal and freeze.

Sugar pack uses little or no liquid, and fruit packed in this way is especially good for cooked dishes such as pies and fruit cocktail. To sugar pack, add "C" to sugar and gently mix with prepared fruit until sugar is dissolved and juice is drawn out of the fruit. Pack, allow head space, seal, and freeze.

Unsweetened pack is the simplest method and the one that keeps the fruit closest to its natural state. It is particularly good for berries such as blueberries, currants, and raspberries. Simply wash and prepare fruit, sprinkle with "C" dissolved in water, pack allowing room for expansion, seal, and freeze.

When the directions call for syrup, prepare it in advance according to the following table:

Type of Syrup	Sugar (cups)	Water (cups)	Yield of Syrup (cups)
30 percent (light)	2	4	5
35 percent	2½	4	5⅓
40 percent (medium)	3	4	5½
50 percent (heavy)	4¾	4	6½
60 percent	7	4	7¾
65 percent	8¾	4	8⅔

For delicately flavored fruits, replace one fourth of the sugar with light corn syrup.

If hot water is used to dissolve the sugar, allow plenty of time for the syrup to cool before use. For best results, chill overnight in the refrigerator.

Add "C" only after the syrup has chilled. The amount recommended is given with instructions for the different fruits (usually from ½ to 1 teaspoon per quart of syrup).

Packaging

Packaging plays an important role in the freezing process. It is essential that you use containers that are highly resistant to moisture and air that can be tightly sealed. Otherwise the food will dry out and become tasteless (and nutritionless). This applies whether you use rigid containers, boilable bags (heat-sealed), or freezer bags (twist-tied).

To make sure that the expansion of the food as it freezes does not break the seal or force off the cover, leave space at the top of the containers. For fruits without liquid, ½ inch of space for a pint or quart container is usually enough. For fruit packed in syrup, more room is necessary, usually 1 inch per quart container.

To keep fruit under the surface of the syrup, place a piece of crumpled parchment paper or other water-resistant wrapping material on top and press down into syrup before closing and sealing the container.

Sliced Apples: Select full-flavored apples that are crisp and firm, not mealy, in texture. Wash, peel, and core. Slice medium apples into twelfths, large ones into sixteenths.

Pack in one of the following ways:

Syrup pack. Use 40 percent syrup. Add 1 teaspoon "C" to each quart of syrup.

To prevent darkening, slice apples directly into cold syrup in containers. Press fruit down in containers and add enough syrup to cover.

Leave head space, seal, and freeze. Pack in one of the following ways:

Sugar pack. To prevent darkening of apples during preparation, slice them into a solution of 2 tablespoons salt to a gallon of water. Hold in this solution no more than 15 to 20 minutes. Drain.

Over each quart (1½ pounds) of apple slices, sprinkle evenly ½ cup of sugar mixed with ¾ teaspoon "C" to prevent darkening. Stir. (Vary sugar according to tartness desired.) Pack apples into containers and press fruit down, leaving head space. Seal and freeze.

Unsweetened pack. Follow directions for sugar pack, omitting sugar.

Applesauce: Select full-flavored apples. Wash apples, peel if desired, core, and slice. To each quart of apple slices add ⅓ cup water; cook until tender. Cool and strain if necessary. Sweeten to taste with ¼ to ¾ cup sugar (or honey) mixed with ¾ teaspoon "C" for each quart (2 pounds) of sauce. Pack into containers, leaving head space. Seal and freeze.

Apricots (High Beta Carotene): Select firm, ripe, uniformly yellow apricots. Sort, wash, halve, and pit. Peel and slice, if desired.

If apricots are not peeled, heat them in boiling water 30 seconds to keep skins from toughening during freezing. Then cool in cold water and drain.

Pack into containers in one of the following ways:

Syrup pack. Use 40 percent syrup, and add 1 teaspoon "C" to each quart of syrup. Pack apricots directly into containers. Cover with syrup and leave head space. Seal and freeze.

Sugar pack. Dissolve ½ teaspoon "C" in ¼ cup cold water, and sprinkle it over one quart of apricots (⅞ pound). Then mix ½ cup sugar with each quart of fruit. Stir until sugar is dissolved. Pack apricots into containers, and press down until fruit is covered with juice, leaving head space. Seal and freeze.

For crushed apricots, select ripe fruit and dip in boiling water for 30 seconds and cool in cold water. Peel the apricots. Pit and crush them coarsely.

For purée, pit and quarter the fruit; press through a sieve. Or heat to boiling point in just enough water to prevent scorching, and then press through a sieve.

With each quart (2 pounds) of prepared apricots, mix ¾ cup sugar or ½ cup honey with ½ teaspoon "C."

Pack into containers, leaving head space. Seal and freeze.

Blackberries, Boysenberries, Dewberries, Lingonberries, Loganberries, Youngberries: Select firm, plump, fully ripe berries with glossy skins. Green berries may cause off-flavor.

Sort and remove any leaves and stems. Wash and drain.

Use one of the three following packs:

Syrup pack. Pack berries into containers and cover with 40 percent or 50 percent syrup, depending on the sweetness of the fruit. Add ¾ teaspoon "C" to each quart of syrup. Pack into containers and leave head space. Seal and freeze.

Sugar pack. To 1 quart (1⅓ pounds) berries, add ¾ cup sugar and ¾ teaspoon "C." Turn berries over and over until most of the sugar is dissolved. Fill containers, leaving head space. Seal and freeze.

For crushed or puréed berries, prepare for packing in the same way as for whole berries. Then crush or press through a sieve for purée. To each quart (2 pounds) of crushed berries or purée add 1 cup sugar (or honey) mixed with ¾ teaspoon "C." Stir until sugar is dissolved; then pack into containers, leaving head space. Seal and freeze.

Unsweetened pack. Pack berries into containers, leaving head space. Seal and freeze.

Sour Cherries: Select bright red, tree-ripened cherries. Stem, sort, and wash thoroughly. Drain and pit.

Use one of the following packs:

Syrup pack. Pack cherries into containers and cover with cold 60 or 65 percent syrup, depending on tartness of the cherries, with 1 teaspoon "C" per quart. Leave head space. Seal and freeze.

Sugar pack. To 1 quart (1⅓ pounds) cherries, add ¾ cup sugar mixed with ¾ teaspoon "C." Mix until sugar is dissolved. Pack into containers, leaving head space. Seal and freeze.

For crushed fruit, prepare for packing as for whole sour cherries. Crush coarsely.

To 1 quart (2 pounds) fruit, add 1 to 1½ cups sugar or 1 cup of honey, depending on sweetness desired, and ½ teaspoon "C." Mix thoroughly until sugar is dissolved. Pack into containers, leaving head space. Seal and freeze.

For puréed berries, select and prepare for packing same as for whole cherries. Then crush berries, heat to boiling point, cool, and press through a sieve.

To 1 quart (2 pounds) fruit purée, add ½ teaspoon "C" and ¾ cup sugar or ½ cup of honey. Pack purée into containers, leaving head space. Seal and freeze.

Sweet Cherries: Sweet cherries should be prepared quickly to avoid color and flavor changes. Red varieties are best for freezing.

Select well-colored, tree-ripened fruit with a sweet flavor. Sort, stem, and wash. Remove pits if desired: they tend to give an almond-like flavor to the fruit. To prevent darkening, drop fruit into "C" syrup as it is being prepared.

Pack in one of the following ways:

Syrup pack. Drain the "C" syrup from the fruit. Pack cherries in containers. Cover with cold "C" syrup (40 percent syrup to which ¾ teaspoon "C" per quart has been added). Leave head space. Seal and freeze.

For sweet and sour cherries, use half sweet cherries and half sour. Pack as above using 50 percent syrup. Add ½ teaspoon "C" per quart.

Cranberries: Choose firm, deep-red berries with glossy skins. Stem and sort. Wash and drain.

Pack in one of the following ways:

Syrup pack. Pack into containers. Cover with cold 50 percent syrup with ½ teaspoon "C" per quart. Leave head space. Seal and freeze.

Sugar pack. For purée, prepare cranberries as for freezing whole. Add 2 cups water to each quart (1 pound) of berries. Cook until skins have popped. Press through a sieve. Add sugar or honey to taste— about 2 cups for each quart (2 pounds) of purée. Stir in ½ teaspoon "C" per quart. Pack into containers, leaving head space. Seal and freeze.

Unsweetened pack. Pack into containers without sugar. Leave head space. Seal and freeze.

Fruit Cocktail: Use any combination of fruits desired . . . sliced or cubed peaches or apricots, melon balls, orange or grapefruit sections, whole seedless grapes, Bing cherries, or pineapple wedges.

Pack into containers, cover with cold 30 to 40 percent syrup, depending on fruits used. Add ½ teaspoon "C" per quart. Leave head space. Seal and freeze.

Grapefruit, Oranges, Nectarines, and Tangerines: You can freeze grapefruit, oranges, nectarines, and tangerines in a 40 percent syrup pack, but we do not go into detail here because all these fruits are readily available year round.

Peaches (High Beta Carotene): Peaches in halves and slices have better quality when packed in syrup or with sugar or honey, but a water pack will serve if sweetening is not desired.

Select firm, ripe peaches with no green color in the skins.

Sort, wash, pit, and peel. For a better product, peel peaches without a boiling-water dip. Slice if desired.

Pack in one of the following ways:

Syrup pack. Use 40 percent syrup, and add ½ teaspoon "C" for each quart of syrup. Put peaches directly into cold syrup in container—starting with ½ cup syrup to a pint container. Press fruit down, and add syrup to cover, leaving head space. Seal and freeze.

Sugar pack. To each quart (1⅓ pounds) of prepared fruit, add ⅔ cup sugar and ½ teaspoon "C." Mix well. Pack into containers, leaving head space. Seal and freeze.

For crushed or puréed fruit, loosen the skins by dipping the peaches in boiling water for ½ to 1 minute. The riper the fruit, the less scalding needed. Cool in cold water, remove skins, and pit. Crush the peaches coarsely. Or, for purée, press through a sieve or heat pitted peaches 4 minutes in just enough water to prevent scorching, and then press through a sieve.

With each quart (2 pounds) of crushed or puréed peaches, mix 1 cup sugar or ¾ cup honey. Add ½ teaspoon "C" to each quart of fruit. Pack into containers, leaving head space. Seal and freeze.

Unsweetened pack. Pack peaches into containers, and cover with cold water containing ½ teaspoon "C" to each quart of water. Leave head space. Seal and freeze.

Pears: Select pears that are well-ripened and firm but not hard. Wash fruit in cold water. Peel, cut in halves or quarters, and remove cores. Pack in one of the following ways:

Syrup pack. Heat pears in boiling 40 percent syrup for 1 to 2 minutes. Drain and cool. Pack pears into containers, and cover with cold 40 percent syrup. For a better product, add ½ teaspoon "C" to a quart of cold syrup. Leave head space. Seal and freeze.

For purée, select well-ripened pears, firm but not hard or gritty. Peel or not, as desired, but do not dip in boiling water to remove skins. Prepare and pack as for peach purée.

Pineapple: Select firm, ripe pineapple with full flavor and aroma. Pare and remove core and eyes. Slice, dice, crush, or cut the pineapple into wedges or sticks.

Pack in one of the following ways:

Syrup pack. Pack fruit tightly into containers. Cover with 30 percent syrup made with pineapple juice, if available, or with water. Leave head space. Seal and freeze.

Unsweetened pack. Pack fruit tightly into containers without sugar. Leave head space. Sprinkle on ½ teaspoon "C."

Raspberries: Raspberries may be frozen in sugar or in syrup or unsweetened. Seedy berries are best for use in making purées or juice.

Select fully ripe, firm, juicy berries. Sort, wash carefully in cold water, and drain thoroughly.

Pack in one of the following ways:

Syrup pack. Put berries into containers, add ¾ teaspoon "C," and cover with cold 40 percent syrup, leaving head space. Seal and freeze.

Sugar pack. To 1 quart (1⅓ pounds) berries, add ¾ cup sugar or honey and ¾ teaspoon "C," and mix thoroughly to avoid crushing. Put into containers, leaving head space. Seal and freeze.

For crushed or puréed berries, prepare as for whole raspberries, then crush or press through a sieve. To 1 quart (2 pounds) crushed berries or purée, add ¾ to 1 cup sugar or honey, depending on sweetness of fruit. Mix until sugar is dissolved. Put into containers, leaving head space. Seal and freeze.

Unsweetened pack. Put berries into containers, leaving head space. Seal and freeze.

Rhubarb: Choose firm, tender, well-colored stalks with good flavor and few fibers. Wash, trim, and cut into 1- or 2-inch pieces or in lengths to fit package. Heating rhubarb in boiling water for 1 minute and cooling promptly in cold water helps retain color and flavor.

Pack in one of the following ways:

Syrup pack. Pack either raw or preheated rhubarb tightly into containers; cover with cold 40 percent syrup. Leave head space. Seal and freeze.

Sugar pack. For purée, prepare rhubarb as for rhubarb stalks or pieces. Add 1 cup water and ½ teaspoon "C" to 1½ quarts (2 pounds) rhubarb, and boil 2 minutes. Cool and press through a sieve. With 1 quart (2 pounds) purée, mix ⅔ cup sugar or ½ cup of honey. Pack into containers, leaving head space. Seal and freeze.

Unsweetened pack. Pack either raw or preheated rhubarb tightly into containers without sugar. Leave head space. Seal and freeze.

Strawberries: Choose firm, ripe, red berries, preferably with a slightly tart flavor. Large berries are better sliced or crushed. Sort berries, wash them in cold water, drain well, and remove hulls.

Sugar and syrup packs make better quality frozen strawberries than berries packed without sweetening.

Pack in one of the following ways:

Syrup pack. Put berries into containers and cover with cold 50 percent syrup with ½ teaspoon "C" per quart. Leave head space. Seal and freeze.

Sugar pack. Add ¾ cup sugar, mixed with ½ teaspoon "C," to 1 quart (1⅓ pounds) strawberries, and mix thoroughly. Put into containers, leaving head space. Seal and freeze.

For sliced or crushed berries, prepare for packing as for whole strawberries; then slice, or crush partially or completely. To 1 quart (1½ pounds) berries add ¾ cup sugar mixed with ½ teaspoon "C"; mix thoroughly. Pack into containers, leaving head space. Seal and freeze.

For purée, prepare strawberries as for freezing whole. Then press berries through a sieve. To 1 quart (2 pounds) purée, add ⅔ cup sugar or ½ cup honey. Add ½ teaspoon "C," and mix well. Put into containers, leaving head space. Seal and freeze.

Unsweetened pack. Pack into containers, leaving head space. For better color, cover with water containing ½ teaspoon "C" to each quart of water. Seal and freeze.

Appendix

Chart of Vitamin C Content

(We have omitted those foods with 2 milligrams or less vitamin C.
Numbered footnotes appear at the end of this chart.)

Fruit and Fruit Products	**Amount**	**Vitamin C (mg)**
Apple juice, fresh or canned	1 cup	2
Apples, raw, about 3 per pound	1 apple	3
Applesauce, canned, sweetened	1 cup	3
Apricots:		
canned in heavy syrup	1 cup	10
cooked, unsweetened, fruit and liquid	1 cup	8
dried, uncooked, 40 halves per cup	1 cup	19
raw, about 12 per pound	3 apricots	10
Apricot nectar, canned	1 cup	8[1]
Avocados, whole fruit, raw:		
California (mid and late winter)		
diameter 3⅝ inches	1 avocado	30
Florida (late summer, fall)		
diameter 3⅝ inches	1 avocado	43
Bananas, raw, medium-sized	1 banana	12
Blackberries, raw	1 cup	30
Blueberries, raw	1 cup	20
Cantaloupes, raw, medium 5-inch		
diameter, about 1⅔ pounds	½ melon	63
Cherries, canned, red, sour, pitted		
water pack	1 cup	12
Cranberry juice cocktail, canned	1 cup	40[2]
Cranberry sauce, sweetened,		
canned, strained	1 cup	6
Fruit cocktail, canned in heavy syrup	1 cup	5
Grapefruit:		
canned, syrup pack	1 cup	76
raw, medium, 3¾-inch		
diameter, white or pink	½ grapefruit	44
Grapefruit juice:		
canned, white:		
unsweetened	1 cup	84
sweetened	1 cup	78
fresh	1 cup	92
frozen concentrate, unsweetened,		
diluted with 3 parts water	1 cup	96

Fruit and Fruit Products	Amount	Vitamin C (mg)
Grapes, raw:		
American type (slip skin)	1 cup	3
European type (adherent skin)	1 cup	6
Lemon juice, raw	1 cup	112
Lemonade concentrate, frozen		
diluted with 4⅓ parts water	1 cup	17
Lemons, raw 2⅛ inch-diameter,		
used for juice	1 lemon	39
Lime juice:		
canned, unsweetened	1 cup	52
fresh	1 cup	79
Limeade concentrate, frozen		
diluted with 4⅓ parts water	1 cup	5
Orange juice:		
canned, unsweetened	1 cup	100
fresh	1 cup	124
frozen concentrate, diluted with		
3 parts water	1 cup	120
Orange-apricot juice drink	1 cup	40[2]
Orange and grapefruit juice,		
frozen concentrate, diluted		
with 3 parts water	1 cup	102
Oranges, raw, 2⅝-inch diameter,		
all commercial varieties	1 orange	66
Papayas, raw, ½-inch cubes	1 cup	102
Peaches:		
canned, yellow-fleshed, solids and liquid:		
syrup pack, heavy, halves sliced	1 cup	7
water pack	1 cup	7
dried, uncooked	1 cup	28
cooked, unsweetened, 10-12		
halves and juice	1 cup	6
frozen, 12-ounce carton, not thawed	1 carton	135[3]
raw:		
sliced	1 cup	12
whole, medium, 2-inch diameter,		
about 4 per pound	1 peach	7
Pears:		
canned, heavy-syrup pack, solids		
and liquids, halves or slices	1 cup	4
raw, 3 by 2½-inch diameter	1 pear	7
Pineapple:		
canned, heavy syrup pack, solids		
and liquids:		
crushed	1 cup	17
slices and juice	2 small or	
	1 large slice	8

Fruit and Fruit Products	Amount	Vitamin C (mg)
raw, diced	1 cup	24
Pineapple juice, canned	1 cup	22
Plums:		
canned, syrup pack (Italian prunes) with pits	1 cup	4
raw, 2-inch diameter, about 2 ounces	1 plum	3
Prune juice, canned or bottled	1 cup	5[1]
Raspberries, red:		
frozen, 10-ounce carton, not thawed	1 carton	59
raw	1 cup	31
Rhubarb, cooked, sugar added	1 cup	17
Strawberries:		
frozen, 10-ounce carton, not thawed	1 carton	150
raw, capped	1 cup	88
Tangerine juice, canned, sweetened	1 cup	55
Tangerines, raw, medium, 2³/₈-inch diameter	1 tangerine	27
Watermelon, raw, wedge, 4 by 8 inches	1 wedge	30

Meat, Poultry, Fish, Shellfish, and Related Products		
Beef and vegetable stew	1 cup	15
Calves' liver	4 ounces	25
Chicken livers, fried	3 medium	20
Clams, raw	3 ounces	8

Vegetables and Vegetable Products		
Artichoke, medium, cooked	1 artichoke	8
Asparagus, green:		
canned, solids and liquid	1 cup	37
cooked, drained:		
pieces, 1½-2 inch lengths	1 cup	38
spears, ½-inch diameter at base	4 spears	16
Basil, fresh	1 cup	27
Beans:		
lima, cooked, drained	1 cup	20
snap, green:		
canned, solids, and liquid	1 cup	10
cooked, drained	1 cup	15
sprouted mung beans, cooked, drained	1 cup	15
yellow or wax:		
canned, solids and liquid	1 cup	12
cooked, drained	1 cup	16
Beet greens, leaves and stems, cooked, drained	1 cup	35

Vegetables and Vegetable Products	Amount	Vitamin C (mg)
Beets:		
canned, solids, and liquid	1 cup	7
cooked, drained, peeled:		
diced or sliced	1 cup	10
whole beets, 2-inch diameter	2 beets	6
Black-eyed peas or cowpeas, cooked	1 cup	28
Broccoli:		
cooked and drained:		
stalks, cut into ½-inch pieces	1 cup	120
whole stalks, medium-sized	1 stalk	162
frozen, chopped from 10-ounce package	1⅜ cup	143
Brussels sprouts, cooked, 7-8		
sprouts per cup	1 cup	97
Cabbage:		
common varieties:		
cooked	1 cup	38
raw:		
coarsely shredded or sliced	1 cup	33
finely shredded or chopped	1 cup	42
celery or Chinese, raw, cut in		
1-inch pieces	1 cup	19
red, raw, coarsely shredded	1 cup	43
Savoy, raw, coarsely shredded	1 cup	39
spoon or Bok-choy, cooked	1 cup	26
Carrots:		
canned, strained or chopped	1 cup	8
cooked and diced	1 cup	9
raw:		
grated	1 cup	9
whole, 5½ by 1 inch	1 carrot	4
Cauliflower, cooked florets	1 cup	66
Celery, raw:		
pieces, diced	1 cup	9
stalk, large outer, 8 by 1½		
inches at root end	1 stalk	4
Chard, steamed, leaves and stalks	1 cup	17
Collards, cooked	1 cup	30
Corn, sweet:		
canned, solids and liquid	1 cup	13
cooked, ear, 5 by 1¾ inches	1 ear	7
Cucumbers, 10 ounce, 7½ by 2 inches:		
raw, pared	1 cucumber	23
raw, pared, center slice ⅛ inch thick	6 slices	6
Dandelion greens, cooked	1 cup	23
Eggplant, steamed	1 cup	5
Endive, curly (including escarole)	2 ounces	6

Vegetables and Vegetable Products	Amount	Vitamin C (mg)
Kale, leaves, including stems, cooked	1 cup	43
Leeks, bulb and lower leaf, sliced	1 cup	17
Lettuce, raw:		
Boston type, 4-inch diameter	1 head	18
Crisphead, as Iceberg, 4¾-inch		
diameter	1 head	29
Loose leaf, or bunching varieties	2 large leaves	9
Mushrooms, canned, solids and liquid	1 cup	4
Mustard greens, cooked	1 cup	38
Okra, pod 3 by ⅝ inch, cooked	8 pods	17
Onions:		
mature:		
raw onion, 2½-inch diameter	1 onion	11
sliced, cooked	1 cup	14
young green, small without tops	6 onions	12
Parsley, raw, chopped	1 tablespoon	7
Parsnips, cooked	1 cup	16
Peas, green:		
canned, solids and liquid	1 cup	22
canned, strained	1 cup	24
cooked	1 cup	33
Peppers, sweet:		
cooked, boiled, drained	1 pod	70
raw, about 5 per pound,		
green pod without stem	1 pod	94
Potato chips, medium, 2-inch diameter	10 chips	3
Potatoes, medium (about 3 per pound, raw):		
baked, peeled after baking	1 potato	20
boiled:		
peeled after boiling	1 potato	22
peeled before boiling	1 potato	20
french-fried, piece 2 by ½		
by ½ inch:		
cooked in deep fat	10 pieces	12
frozen, heated	10 pieces	12
mashed:		
milk added	1 cup	19
milk and butter added	1 cup	18
Pumpkin, canned	1 cup	12
Radishes, raw, small without tops	4 radishes	10
Rutabagas, diced	⅔ cup	21
Sauerkraut, canned, solids and liquid	1 cup	33
Spinach:		
canned, drained solids	1 cup	24
cooked	1 cup	35

Vegetables and Vegetable Products	Amount	Vitamin C (mg)
Squash, cooked:		
summer, diced	1 cup	21
winter, baked, mashed	1 cup	27
Sweet potatoes, medium (5 by 2 inches, weight raw about 6 ounces):		
baked, peeled after baking	1 sweet potato	24
boiled, peeled after boiling	1 sweet potato	25
candied, 3½ by 2¼ inches	1 sweet potato	17
canned, vacuum or solid pack	1 cup	30
Tomato catsup	1 cup	41
Tomatoes:		
canned, solids and liquid	1 cup	41
raw, approximately 3-inch diameter, weight 7 ounces	1 tomato	42
Tomato juice, canned	1 cup	39
Turnip greens, cooked	1 cup	40
Watercress, leaf and stem, raw	1 cup	15
Zucchini, cooked	1 cup	21

Notes:
[1]This is the amount from the fruit. Additional ascorbic acid may be added by the manufacturer. Refer to the label for this information.
[2]Value listed is based on products with label stating 30 milligrams per 6 fluid ounce serving.
[3]This value includes ascorbic acid added by manufacturer.

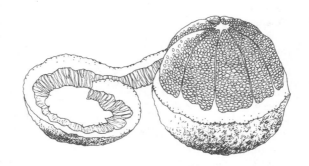

Chart of Vitamin E Content

Vegetables & Legumes	Amount	Vitamin E (mg)
Asparagus, fresh	½ cup	1.3
Asparagus, cooked	½ cup	2.5
Beans:		
Black Beans, cooked	1 cup	1.0
Great Northern Beans, cooked	1 cup	2.0
Kidney Beans, cooked	1 cup	1.2
Lima Beans, cooked	1 cup	3.0
Navy Beans, cooked	1 cup	2.1
Pinto Beans, cooked	1 cup	0.9
Garbanzo Beans (chick peas), cooked	1 cup	1.9
Beet Greens, cooked	½ cup	1.2
Broccoli, cooked	½ cup	1.9
Dandelion Greens, fresh	1 cup	1.4
cooked	1 cup	2.4
Lentils, cooked	1 cup	1.2
Mustard Greens, fresh	1 cup	1.1
Green Peas & Pods, fresh	1 cup	3.9
Pumpkin, cooked	½ cup	0.8
Spinach, fresh	1 cup	1.5
Squash		
Acorn, baked	½ cup	0.8
Butternut, baked	½ cup	0.8
Sweet Potato, baked	1 medium	5.6
Turnip Greens, cooked	½ cup	1.2
Oils		
Canola Oil	1 tablespoon	7.9
Cod Liver Oil	1 tablespoon	3.1
Corn Oil	1 tablespoon	12.5
Cottonseed Oil	1 tablespoon	7.8
Olive Oil	1 tablespoon	1.6
Peanut Oil	1 tablespoon	2.3
Safflower Oil	1 tablespoon	4.6
Sesame Oil	1 tablespoon	3.5
Soybean Oil	1 tablespoon	12.5
Sunflower Oil	1 tablespoon	7.6
Salad Dressing		
1000 Island, regular	1 tablespoon	5.0
Blue Cheese	1 tablespoon	1.1
French, regular	1 tablespoon	4.4
Italian, regular	1 tablespoon	4.4
Ranch, regular	1 tablespoon	2.5
Vinegar & Oil, regular	1 tablespoon	3.0

Fruits	**Amount**	**Vitamin E (mg)**
Avocado, California	1 each	2.3
Florida	1 each	4.1
Blueberries, fresh	1 cup	2.7
Currants, fresh	1 cup	1.1
Fruit Cocktail	1 cup	2.2
Mandarin Oranges	1 cup	1.3
Mango	1 each	2.3

Cereals		
Ralston, cooked	1 cup	1.4
Wheatena, cooked	1 cup	1.4
Brown Rice, cooked	1 cup	1.4
Oat Bran	1 tablespoon	0.4
Rice Bran	1 tablespoon	0.9
Wheat germ	1 tablespoon	1.0
Wheat germ, toasted	1 tablespoon	1.9

Fish		
Crab, cooked	1 cup	1.2
Mackerel	3½ ounces	1.5
Oysters	1 cup	2.0
Salmon, broiled	3 ounces	1.3
Sole, baked	3½ ounces	1.6

Nuts		
Almonds, dried	¼ cup	7.5
Cashews	¼ cup	2.6
Filberts	¼ cup	8.1
Macadamias	¼ cup	5.1
Peanuts, dried	¼ cup	3.7
Sunflower Seeds, dried	¼ cup	7.3
Walnuts, English	¼ cup	1.0

Chart of Beta Carotene Content

Vegetables *(from plant sources)*	Amount	mcg
Beet greens, cooked	1 cup	7,340
Broccoli, raw	½ cup	1,360
cooked	1 cup	2,460
Cabbage, Bok-choy, raw	1 cup	2,100
Bok-choy, cooked	1 cup	4,370
Savoy, cooked	1 cup	1,290
Carrots, cooked	½ cup	16,035
Carrot juice	½ cup	63,300
Chard, Swiss, raw	1 cup	2,590
cooked	1 cup	11,980
Chicory greens, raw	½ cup	3,600
Collard greens, raw	1 cup	1,200
cooked	1 cup	3,200
Dandelion greens, raw	1 cup	7,700
cooked	1 cup	12,290
Dock (sorrel greens), raw	1 cup	5,320
cooked	1 cup	3,470
Kale, raw	1 cup	5,960
cooked	1 cup	8,940
Mustard greens, raw	1 cup	2,970
cooked	1 cup	5,475
Onion, spring, chopped	½ cup	2,500
Peas, green, young tender, raw	1 cup	1,340
Peppers, jalapeno, canned	½ cup	1,160
Red chili, fresh	½ cup	8,060
Sweet red, raw	½ cup	2,850
Pimiento, canned	2 ounces	1,310
Spinach, cooked	½ cup	8,765
Squash, winter		
Acorn, baked	1 cup	1,050
Butternut, baked	1 cup	17,150
Hubbard, baked	1 cup	14,500
Sweet potato	1 small	25,315
Tomato, raw	1 cup	2,040
Turnip greens, cooked	½ cup	5,250
Vegetable juice cocktail	1 cup	2,830
Fruits		
Apricots, fresh	3 each	1,660
canned	3 each	1,240
Apricot nectar	1 cup	3,300
Cantaloupe, cubed	½ cup	2,580
Cherries, sour, canned	1 cup	1,840

Fruits	**Amount**	**mcg**
Mango	½ cup	3,210
Passion fruit juice, yellow	1 cup	5,950
Pumpkin, canned	½ cup	27,000
Persimmons	1 each	2,375
Tangerine juice	1 cup	1,240

1 RE (Retinol Equivalent) = 1 mcg retinol = 6 mcg beta carotene
1 RE = 10 IU of beta carotene (from plant sources)

Index

References

1. Cooper, Kenneth H., M.D., *Antioxidant Revolution*. Nashville, Thomas Nelson Publishers, 1994.

2. USDA Home & Garden Bulletin Number 72, "Nutritive Value of Foods." Service, U.S. Department of Agriculture, Washington, D.C., 1986.

3. Adams, Catherine F., Agricultural Handbook No. 456, "Nutritive Value of American Foods in Common Units," USDA Agricultural Research Service, USDA, Washington, D.C., 1975.

4. National Dairy Council, *Newer Knowledge of Cheese*. Rosemont, IL. National Dairy Council, 1986.

5. Agricultural Research Service, U.S. Dept. Agriculture. "Composition of Foods," Agricultural Handbooks 8-1 through 8-14. Washington D.C., U.S. Government Printing Office, 1989.

6. Whitney, E. R. & Boyle, M. A., *Understanding Nutrition*. Fourth Edition, New York, West Publishing Company, 1994.

7. William, S. R., *Nutrition and Diet Therapy*, Sixth Edition. St. Louis, Times Mirror/Mosby College Publishing, 1993.

8. Netzer, C. T., *The Complete Book of Food Counts*, Third Edition. New York. Bantam Doubleday Dell Publishing Group, Incorporated, 1994.

9. "Vitamin A Activity of Selected Fruits," C D Johnson. R. R. Eitenmiller, PhD., D.A. Lillard, PhD. and M. Rao. Vol. 85, No. 1627, December 1985.

10. Pennington, J. A. T., J.P. Lippincot, *Bowes and Church's Food Values of Portions Commonly Used:* Philadelphia, 1994.

11. "Vitamin E Content of Foods," P. J. McLaughlin, PhD., and John L. Weihrauch, *Journal of the American Dietetic Association*; Vol. 75, No. 647, 1979.

12. "Tocopherols in Foods and Fats," Hal T. Sloder, *Lipids*, Vol. 65, No. 291, 1971.

13. Hands, Elizabeth S., *Food Finder*, Third Edition, ESHA Research, Salem, OR, 1990.